When Children Don't Sleep Well

✔ Programs *That Work*™

When Children Don't Sleep Well

INTERVENTIONS FOR PEDIATRIC SLEEP DISORDERS

Therapist Guide

V. Mark Durand

UNIVERSITY PRESS

2008

OXFORD
UNIVERSITY PRESS

Oxford University Press, Inc., publishes works that further
Oxford University's objective of excellence
in research, scholarship, and education.

Oxford   New York
Auckland   Cape Town   Dar es Salaam   Hong Kong   Karachi
Kuala Lumpur   Madrid   Melbourne   Mexico City   Nairobi
New Delhi   Shanghai   Taipei   Toronto

With offices in
Argentina   Austria   Brazil   Chile   Czech Republic   France   Greece
Guatemala   Hungary   Italy   Japan   Poland   Portugal   Singapore
South Korea   Switzerland   Thailand   Turkey   Ukraine   Vietnam

Copyright © 2008 by Oxford University Press, Inc.

Published by Oxford University Press, Inc.
198 Madison Avenue, New York, New York 10016

www.oup.com

Library of Congress Cataloging-in-Publication Data
Durand, Vincent Mark.
When children don't sleep well : interventions for pediatric sleep disorders :
therapist guide / V. Mark Durand.
p. ; cm. — (ProgramsThatWork)
Includes bibliographical references.
ISBN 978-0-19-532947-6 (pbk. : alk. paper)   1. Sleep disorders in children—Treatment.   I. Title.   II. Series: Treatments that work. [DNLM:
1. Sleep Disorders—therapy.   2. Child. WM 188 D949w 2008]
RJ506.S55D88 2008
618.92′8498—dc22   2007046109

9 8 7 6 5 4 3 2 1

Printed in the United States of America
on acid-free paper

About Programs *ThatWork*™

Stunning developments in healthcare have taken place over the last several years, but many of our widely accepted interventions and strategies in mental health and behavioral medicine have been brought into question by research evidence as not only lacking benefit but perhaps inducing harm. Other strategies have been proven effective using the best current standards of evidence, resulting in broad-based recommendations to make these practices more available to the public. Several recent developments are behind this revolution. First, we have arrived at a much deeper understanding of pathology, both psychological and physical, which has led to the development of new, more precisely targeted interventions. Second, our increased understanding of developmental issues allows a finer matching of interventions to developmental levels. Third, our research methodologies have improved substantially, such that we have reduced threats to internal and external validity, making the outcomes more directly applicable to clinical situations. Fourth, governments around the world and healthcare systems and policymakers have decided that the quality of care should improve, that it should be evidence-based, and that it is in the public's interest to ensure that this happens (Barlow, 2004; Institute of Medicine, 2001).

Of course, the major stumbling block for clinicians everywhere is the accessibility of newly developed evidence-based psychological interventions. Workshops and books can go only so far in acquainting responsible and conscientious practitioners with the latest behavioral healthcare practices and their applicability to individual patients. This new series, Programs *ThatWork*™, is devoted to communicating these exciting new interventions to clinicians on the frontlines of practice.

The manuals and workbooks in this series contain step-by-step detailed procedures for assessing and treating specific problems and diagnoses.

But this series also goes beyond the books and manuals by providing ancillary materials that will approximate the supervisory process in assisting practitioners in the implementation of these procedures in their practice.

In our emerging healthcare system, the growing consensus is that evidence-based practice offers the most responsible course of action for the mental health professional. All behavioral healthcare clinicians deeply desire to provide the best possible care for their patients. In this series, our aim is to close the dissemination and information gap and make that possible.

This therapist guide, and the workbook for parents, addresses pediatric sleep problems. Sleep difficulties are quite common among children, but they are not a normal part of growing up. Sleep problems can affect children's daily functioning and can also be very disruptive to families. Medications are regularly prescribed for children's sleep problems, however their safety and effectiveness in children has not been established. This guide outlines proven methods for improving children's sleep without the use of drugs.

Specific interventions target a wide range of sleep problems that affect children. This comprehensive guide uses an easy to follow modular format to systematically address a child's sleep issues. It provides the therapist with detailed procedures for working with parents. The parent workbook includes step-by-step instruction for carrying out nighttime interventions. This program can be used to manage multiple sleep issues or as part of treatment for other disorders. Clinicians will find this an indispensable resource.

David H. Barlow, Editor-in-Chief,
Programs *ThatWork*™
Boston, Massachusetts

References

Barlow, D. H. (2004). Psychological treatments. *American Psychologist, 59*, 869–878.

Institute of Medicine (2001). *Crossing the quality chasm: A new health system for the 21st century*. Washington, DC: National Academy Press.

Acknowledgements

A number of students over the years—including Jodi Mindell, Eileen Merges, Peter Gernert-Dott, and Kristin Christodulu—guided and directed this work and I am deeply indebted to them. Each has gone on to distinguish themselves in academic and clinical careers and I am proud to have been a part of their educational experience. The developmental editor for this book—Julia TerMaat—helped wrestle and make sense of a tremendous amount of information that went into these plans and I truly appreciate her patience and guidance. More than two decades ago my son Jonathan was born and his sleep problems motivated a line of research that I hoped would bring some help for other parents. Now a young man, his strength, character, humor, and intelligence are still an inspiration.

Contents

Module 5: Nightmares and Sleep Terrors

Module 6: Bedwetting

Module 7: Other Sleep-Related Issues

Introductory Information for Therapists

Background Information and Purpose of This Program

This book is designed as a general resource for therapists, covering a wide range of common sleep problems and presenting a variety of treatment options. Contrary to popular belief, sleep problems are not usually "outgrown," and without treatment, can continue for years. Intervention is essential for the child as well as for the family. Sleep disturbances in children can be among the most disruptive problems faced by families. Not only can sleep problems negatively impact a child's mood and cognitive functioning, but they can also disrupt the sleep of family members and affect the entire family. As a result of the high comorbidity with other disorders, clinicians are often faced with a family that—because of sleep deprivation—may be less able to participate in therapy.

Sleep problems result from a combination of complex biological, cognitive, and psychological influences and therefore require accurate assessment to design appropriate treatments. This program provides straightforward tools for assessing sleep disorders and outlines interventions for specific problems. Children often suffer from more than one sleep problem, and this program can be used to address multiple problems simultaneously or one by one. This program can also be used in conjunction with treatment for other non-sleep problems, as sleep-related difficulties often accompany many childhood disorders. The Adaptations chapter addresses sleep issues particular to certain disorders.

Rather than treat the child directly, this program targets parents, as they are the ones who must carry out the nighttime interventions. In the case of older children who can take an active role in treatment, parents are instead heavily involved in monitoring the plan. Therapists and parents work closely together to identify the child's sleep problem and create an intervention plan. Intervention plans are individualized to suit the child's problem. Equally as important, the program outlines how to adapt plans to meet the specific needs of each family, since not all families are willing or capable of carrying out all types of interventions.

Information on Sleep Disorders

Sleep disorders include "routine" problems such as bedtime disturbances, night waking, nightmares, and sleep terrors, but can also involve more complex problems such as those associated with breathing (e.g., apnea) and limb movement problems (e.g., restless legs syndrome). The prevalence of sleep problems varies somewhat with age. Bedtime problems and night waking occurs among almost 40% of infants and in 25% to 50% of preschoolers; bedtime resistance is observed in 15% to 27% of school-aged children (Owens, Rosen, & Mindell, 2003). These percentages increase for children with special needs. For example, 25% to 50% of school-aged children and adolescents with attention-deficit hyperactivity disorder (ADHD) display difficulty initiating and maintaining sleep (Owens, 2005). Up to 80% of children with pervasive developmental disorders (including autism) are reported by parents as having significantly disturbed sleep (Durand, 1998). Although long-term follow-up studies are not available, it is generally assumed that the vulnerability for continued sleep disturbances follows children into adulthood.

Disorder or Problem Focus

The program presented in this manual is designed for use with children of all ages, although usually no intervention is typically recommended for children before 6 months old. The therapist does not provide direct intervention to the child for most sleep problems. Instead, parents or caregivers are trained to implement the plans at home. Sleep disorders may be the child's primary or secondary problem (see the Adaptations chapter for more information on comorbidity) and may be a result of psychological or biological factors. Several sleep problems such as hypersomnia or narcolepsy, or breathing-related disorders such as apnea, require medical intervention. For these kinds of disorders, evaluation at a sleep center is recommended.

The complex nature of sleep disorders calls for practitioners to have a broad clinical background. To be successful when assessing and treating sleep problems, professionals need training in how to design and implement behavioral interventions as well as an understanding of the nature of these disorders—including biological influences. For example, if a child has difficulty waking up in the morning, this could be the result of a number of factors including simply unreported night waking, interrupted breathing during sleep, or a limb movement disorder. Although clinicians need not be experts in every area, they do need to be aware of all possible causes of sleep disturbances.

Diagnostic Criteria for Pediatric Sleep Problems

Sleep disorders are divided into two major categories: dyssomnias and parasomnias. Dyssomnias involve difficulties in getting enough sleep, problems with sleeping when one wants to, and complaints about the quality of sleep, such as not feeling refreshed even though one has slept the whole night. The parasomnias are characterized by abnormal behavioral or physiological events that occur during sleep, such as nightmares and sleepwalking. The following table lists the sleep disorders covered in the DSM-IV-TR.

Essential to a diagnosis of a sleep disorder is an assessment of daytime sequelae, or the impact on the child's behavior while awake. For example, if it takes a child 90 minutes to fall asleep at night, but this doesn't bother him or her and the child feels rested during the day, then no disorder is present. However, if this delay is anxiety provoking and the child is fatigued the next day, then this would be considered a sleep problem. It is to some degree a subjective decision, dependent in part on how the child and the family perceive the situation and react to it.

Development of This Treatment Program and Evidence Base

This program was developed at the University at Albany, State University of New York, in the mid 1980s. The initial impetus was personal—

Table 1.1 DSM-IV-TR Sleep Disorders

Sleep Disorder	Description
Dyssomnias (Disturbances in the amount, timing, or quality of sleep.)	
Primary Insomnia	Difficulty initiating or maintaining sleep, or sleep that is not restorative (not feeling rested even after normal amounts of sleep).
Primary Hypersomnia	Complaint of excessive sleepiness that is displayed as either prolonged sleep episodes or daytime sleep episodes.
Narcolepsy	Irresistible attacks of refreshing sleep occurring daily, accompanied by episodes of brief loss of muscle tone (cataplexy).
Breathing-Related Sleep Disorder	Sleep disruption caused by breathing difficulties, leading to excessive sleepiness or insomnia.
Circadian Rhythm Sleep Disorder (Sleep-Wake Schedule Disorder)	Persistent or recurrent sleep disruption due to a mismatch between the sleep-wake schedule required by a person's environment and his or her circadian sleep-wake pattern. This disruption leads to excessive sleepiness or insomnia.
Parasomnias (Disturbances in arousal and sleep stage transition that interfere with the sleep process.)	
Nightmare Disorder (Dream Anxiety Disorder)	Repeated awakenings with detailed recall of extended and extremely frightening dreams, usually involving threats to survival, security, or self-esteem. The awakenings generally occur during the second half of the sleep cycle.
Sleep Terror Disorder	Recurrent episodes of abrupt disturbance during sleep, usually occurring during the first third of the major sleep episode and beginning with a panicky scream.
Sleepwalking Disorder	Repeated episodes of arising from bed during sleep and walking about, usually occurring during the first third of the major sleep episode.

Source: American Psychiatric Association (2000). *The Diagnostic and Statistical Manual of Mental Disorders* (4th ed.). Arlington, VA: American Psychiatric Press.

the multiple sleep problems displayed by the author's own young son and the relative lack of intervention options available to families at that time. The author, along with then–doctoral student Dr. Jodi A. Mindell, began a series of studies exploring a range of behavioral interventions for pediatric sleep disturbances.

From the beginning, we conceptualized sleep disorders from an integrative perspective, which includes several assumptions (Durand, Mindell, Mapstone, & Gernert-Dott, 1998). The first is that, at some level, both biological and psychological factors are present in most cases. A second assumption is that these multiple factors are reciprocally related. For example, Adair and colleagues (1991) observed that children who woke frequently at night often fell asleep in the presence of parents. However, they also noted that child temperament may have played a role in this arrangement, because these children had comparatively difficult temperaments, and their parents were presumably present in order to attend to sleep-initiation difficulties. In other words, personality characteristics, sleep difficulties, and parental reaction interact in a reciprocal manner to produce and maintain sleep problems.

Some children are biologically vulnerable to disturbed sleep. This vulnerability differs and can range from mild to more severe disturbances. For example, a child may be a light sleeper (easily aroused at night) or have a family history of insomnia, narcolepsy, or obstructed breathing. All these factors can contribute to eventual sleeping problems. Such influences have been referred to as predisposing conditions (Spielman & Glovinsky, 1991); they may not, by themselves, always cause problems, but they may combine with other factors to interfere with sleep. Biological vulnerability may, in turn, interact with sleep stress (Durand et al., 1995), which includes a number of events that can negatively affect sleep. For example, poor bedtime habits (such as having too much caffeine) can interfere with falling asleep. Although we may intuitively assume that biological factors come first, extrinsic influences such as poor sleep hygiene (the daily activities that affect how we sleep) can affect the physiological activity of sleep. And, whether disturbances continue or become more severe may depend on how they are managed.

Our early studies focused on validating interventions for individual child problems, such as bedtime disturbances or night waking, using single subject methodologies. For example, we, and others, assessed an alternative to extinction that is often recommended for bedtime disturbances—graduated extinction (Durand & Mindell, 1990; Rolider & Van Houten, 1984). We expanded this approach to include the treatment of children who displayed multiple sleep problems—bedtime disturbances and disruptive night waking. A combination of interventions was used to improve the bedtime problems, including establishing bedtime routines and using graduated extinction (gradually fading attention to tantrums) (Mindell & Durand, 1993). This package of treatments was successful in reducing the bedtime disturbances of all of the children, and importantly, also resulted in a near elimination of night waking. Although night waking was not specifically targeted, the improvement of bedtime disturbances appeared to lead to improvements in this second sleep disturbance.

A series of studies followed that focused on the treatment of sleep disturbance in children with special needs such as autism (Christodulu & Durand, 2004; Durand & Christodulu, 2004; Durand, Gernert-Dott, & Mapstone, 1996). In addition to studying varying populations, we explored behavioral interventions for one of the parasomnias—sleep terror disorder. Our approach to reducing chronic sleep terrors is the use of scheduled awakenings. In the first controlled study of its kind, we instructed parents of children who were experiencing almost nightly sleep terrors to awaken their child briefly approximately 30 minutes before a typical episode (Durand & Mindell, 1999). This simple technique, which was faded out over several weeks, was successful in almost completely eliminating these disturbing events. We later demonstrated the effectiveness of this approach with children with autism who also exhibited sleep terrors (Durand, 2002).

Limits and Benefits of This Treatment Program

A good night's sleep is essential to a child's well-being. Furthermore, an improvement in a child's sleep and nighttime behavior often results in increased parent satisfaction. Most of the interventions outlined in this book show results within a matter of weeks. Although it is not uncommon for sleep problems to reoccur (for example, if there are changes in sleep schedules), reinstating the intervention often quickly resolves the problem.

The manual provides choices of interventions based on child sleep problems as well as family need. All of the intervention plans have limitations. For example, graduated extinction—an approach that involves some level of ignoring the cries of the children—is difficult for many parents who have emotional reactions to their child's tantrums. On the other hand, sleep restriction—where the child is initially kept up later and sleeps less—results in fewer instances of child disruption, but also requires families to monitor the child later into the evening. We advise weighing the pros and cons of each approach with families prior to implementation.

A possible drawback of this program is that therapists must rely on parents for information about the child's sleep problem and the intervention's effectiveness; however, our experience indicates that parents are a reliable source. Moreover, parent adherence is critical to successful implementation of the intervention. Since parents' preferences are taken into account when selecting an intervention, their adherence is more likely.

The Role of Medications

Although medication use is often the approach of choice of pediatricians when faced with a child sleep problem, medication is not recommended as a long-term solution for the majority of sleep problems, especially in children (Mindell, Emslie, Blumer, Genel, Glaze, Ivanenko, et al., 2006). According to most sleep professionals, medication is usually recommended only as a short-term answer to adult sleep problems, and rarely as an intervention for children. That being said, many children continue to receive a variety of prescribed (e.g., clonidine, trazodone (Desyrel®), zolpidem (Ambien®), zaleplon (Sonata®) and over-the-counter (e.g., diphenhydramine Benadryl®, melatonin) medications to help them sleep better.

Concerns about creating dependence and building tolerance are primary for consideration of medication use. An additional problem with some medications is "insomnia rebound," where not only does the sleep difficulty come back after the person stops taking the medication, it comes back worse than before. What typically transpires is that the person tries to stop taking the medication, but the sleep problems return in a more severe form, so the person's reaction is to go back to taking medication. This vicious cycle can be extremely difficult to break out of once it has begun.

Because many children come to our program already taking some form of medication—for example, Benadryl® or melatonin—the decision about whether or not to continue its use is necessary. This decision is made with the family and the family's physician. We typically require a waiver from the pediatrician prior to recommending any changes in medication. Titration of medication typically occurs only after the plan is implemented and an evaluation strategy is in place to assess the effects of removing medication.

Outline of This Treatment Program

The first step of this program is an assessment of the child's sleep problems using the Albany Sleep Problems Scale (ASPS). In addition, parents are instructed to keep a Sleep Diary and a Behavior Log. Before treatment begins, it is also essential to assess the family's ability to carry out specific kinds of interventions using the Sleep Intervention Questionnaire (SIQ).

After assessment and treatment planning, the Decision-Tree in Module 1 directs to intervention modules for specific problems. Each module chapter outlines a first session and follow-up sessions for intervention.

Regardless of the sleep problem, we recommend starting with Module 2: Good Sleep Hygiene. Sometimes establishing good sleep habits and a bedtime routine is all that is needed to resolve the child's sleep problem.

Module 3: Bedtime offers two interventions for bedtime disturbances: graduated extinction and bedtime fading. The therapist and parents compare the two methods and decide together which is most suitable for the family's situation.

The interventions in Module 4: Night Waking include sleep restriction, graduated extinction, and scheduled awakening. An intervention is selected depending on whether the child's waking is disruptive or nondisruptive, and the preferences of the parents.

Module 5: Nightmares and Sleep Terrors targets these different, but commonly confused sleep problems. For nightmares, the use of "magic," relaxation, and paradoxical intention are recommended depending on the child's age. Sleep terrors are handled by increasing the amount of sleep the child gets, or implementing scheduled awakening.

Though not a sleep problem per se, bedwetting is addressed in Module 6. It outlines the "bell and the pad" technique, dry bed training, and full-spectrum home training. The use of medication for treating bedwetting is also discussed.

Module 7 provides information on other sleep-related issues, such as sleepwalking and sleeping at the wrong times. It explores the causes of excessive sleepiness, including hypersomnia and narcolepsy, breathing-related sleep disorders, and limb movement disorders. The impact of anxiety and depression on sleep is also discussed. Finally, this module touches on sleep-related headaches, rhythmic movement disorder, and teeth-grinding.

The Adaptations chapter offers suggestions on age-related concerns and addresses treating children with specific disorders, such as autism or ADHD. It also outlines how to treat parents' sleep disorders along with the child's.

Fidelity checklists have been included in an appendix. Each checklist includes an outline of the corresponding module and space for notes. Therapists may want to use these as part of the supervision process or to rate self-adherence. These forms may be photocopied from the book as needed.

Overview of Sleep

It is important to understand the phenomenon of sleep as it serves as the basis for understanding disturbed sleep. During sleep the brain is not "shut off," but is instead going through much the same type of cyclical process as when one is awake. This cycle of sleep is divided into two broad categories: rapid eye movement or REM sleep (what we commonly refer to as dream sleep), and non-rapid eye movement or NREM sleep

(Hauri, 1982). The brain cycles through these stages of sleep throughout the night in a pattern that is similar among all human beings.

Stages of Sleep

The NREM sleep is usually divided into four stages (referred to as stages 1–4), and these stages are based on different brain wave patterns seen during different points in NREM sleep. The stages of sleep roughly correspond to how deeply we sleep. For example, stage 1 represents "light" sleep, stage 2 "deeper" sleep, and stages 3 and 4 the "deepest" levels of sleep. Stage 1 sleep is a transitional stage between sleep and wakefulness. People tend to feel that they are awake during this time, although their thoughts begin to drift; in research where volunteers had their eyes taped open, they couldn't recall pictures presented to them while they were in this sleep stage (Rechtschaffen & Foulkes, 1965). As the brain runs through its cycle and shifts back from the deeper stages of sleep into the light sleep of stage 1, we also experience what are called "partial arousals" or "partial wakenings" (Anch, Browman, Mitler, & Walsh, 1988). Difficulties during this transition in sleep stages appear at least partially responsible for night waking among children as well as adults.

Stage 2 is the first true sleep state and includes two characteristic brain wave patterns called sleep spindles and K-complexes. Because they are very similar, researchers often consider sleep stages 3 and 4 together and refer to them collectively as "slow wave" or "delta sleep" (for the type of brain wave pattern), or deep sleep. It is very difficult to awaken someone from this stage of sleep, and even if successful, it can take some time before the person is fully alert. Sleep begins in NREM sleep and progresses through stages 1 through 4, with a complete "cycle" of the four stages of NREM sleep taking about 90 minutes in adults and about 60 minutes in infants (Hauri, 1982).

A number of the sleep disorders that people experience occur primarily during NREM sleep. A partial list of these NREM sleep disorders includes sleepwalking, sleep terrors, and sleep bruxism (teeth-grinding during sleep) (Giles & Buysse, 1993). The purpose of NREM sleep is still unknown, although some preliminary research indicates that one function of these states of sleep may be related to our immune system—possibly signaling the rebuilding of this system (Blakeslee, 1993; Palmblad, Petrini, Wasserman, & Akerstedt, 1979).

Following this progression of sleep stages (from stages 1 to 4), the brain transitions to rapid eye movement, or REM sleep. This is the period of time when we dream. Our eyes periodically move in a rapid succession during this time, yet our body is "atonic," or does not move. REM sleep is often characterized as a time where the brain is active but the body is not; in contrast, NREM sleep can be characterized as a time during sleep when our brain is relatively inactive, but our body is not. The brain progresses through NREM and REM stages of sleep several times throughout the night (Carskadon & Dement, 1989).

Some sleep disturbances occur primarily during REM sleep. Nightmares, for example, are reported when people are in this sleep stage. In addition, another predominantly REM sleep phenomenon is called sleep paralysis, and it involves the inability to move arms or legs, and is often accompanied by brief but intense fear. A number of the other disorders occur during either NREM or REM sleep, and include urination while asleep (sleep enuresis), snoring, and sleeptalking.

Sleep Needs

A "normal" amount of sleep varies considerably from person to person; for some people, 5–6 hours of sleep per night is enough to be fully rested, whereas others may need as much as 9 hours of sleep per night. Sleep needs also change as we age. Infants sleep as much as 16½ hours per day, while college-aged students sleep an average of 7–8 hours per day.

Sleep Schedules

Sleep is part of a complex set of biological events that change over the course of a day-and-night cycle. The sleep-wake cycle is considered one of the circadian rhythms that is controlled by the superchiasmatic nucleus (SCN)—our "biological clock." The SCN is located on top of the main junction of nerve fibers that connects to our eyes, a connection that becomes important especially for sleep. The SCN seems to signal our brain when it is time to sleep and when it is time to be awake, and this sleep-wake cycle runs through its course over a period of about 24 hours. The light provided by the sun appears to serve as a timekeeper, synching our brain with the day by triggering the production of melatonin. When this system is not working properly, sleep-wake schedule disorders can occur, and seriously interfere with a child's sleep.

Within this cycle, people vary in how they respond, with "larks" showing a biological preference for early mornings and early evenings, and "owls" tending to wake up later in the morning and fall asleep later in the evening. These patterns are independent of environmental events.

Use of the Parent Workbook

The corresponding workbook aids parents in implementing this program for their child. Every chapter of the workbook corresponds to a module of treatment as outlined in this guide. Each chapter describes options for intervention to be discussed with the therapist. It then provides parents with step-by-step instruction for carrying out specific interventions. The workbook also includes assessment tools and monitoring forms. (Additional copies of forms can be photocopied from the workbook as needed.)

Since parents must act as the "primary therapist" with their child, use of the workbook helps ensure their active participation. Stress to parents that their persistence is crucial to successful intervention of their child's sleep problem. As children with sleep problems often relapse, the workbook is a valuable resource for parents to refer to after therapy has ended. It can also be used to address parents' own sleep issues.

Module 1
Pre-Intervention Assessment and Planning

First Session

Sleep Interview and Assessment Tools

(Corresponds to chapter 1 and 2 of the workbook)

Materials Needed

- The Albany Sleep Problems Scale (ASPS)
- Sleep Diary
- Behavior Log

Outline

- Set agenda
- Provide information about sleep and its problems
- Administer the Albany Sleep Problems Scale (ASPS)
- Introduce Sleep Diary and Behavior Log
- Assign homework

Setting the Agenda

Provide the family with an overview of the session. Discuss expectations for future sessions and general expectations for homework. Explain to the parents how they will be the primary therapist for their child, since they may be expecting you to "fix" their child's sleep problem. Many parents look to sleep professionals to suggest a treatment—such as with medication—that involves minimal effort on their part.

Families will be provided readings in the workbook on the nature of sleep and its disorders. Give a general overview in the first session to clarify that:

■ Sleep is affected by biology as well as environmental influences

■ Sleep problems are very common among children as well as adults

■ There are a number of interventions that can be helpful, although sometimes sleep problems are not "cured" but managed

Albany Sleep Problems Scale

The Albany Sleep Problems Scale (ASPS) can be used to help identify the nature of a child's sleep problem. A copy of the ASPS is provided as an appendix. Typically, much of this information would be assessed through an overnight polysomnographic assessment in a sleep laboratory. Unfortunately, many sleep labs will not conduct these assessments with young children because of practical difficulties. When this is the case, the ASPS is used to help gather information for an appropriate identification of the sleep problem and its causes.

The ASPS is administered either as a structured interview or self-administered by family members. It helps the clinician explore a wide range of influences affecting sleep. This sleep problems scale highlights problems that may be the result of insomnia (difficulty initiating, maintaining, or gaining from sleep), hypersomnia (excessive sleepiness), narcolepsy (irresistible attacks of sleep), breathing-related sleep disorders, circadian rhythm sleep disorders (sleep difficulties due to a mismatch between the sleep-wake schedule desired and the current schedule), nightmares, sleep terrors (a disruption in sleep that begins with a panicky scream), as well as other sleep difficulties.

The questions found on this instrument follow, along with instructions for obtaining additional information in this manual. See ASPS in appendix for 0–4 score key.

Sleep Hygiene Questions

1. Does the child have a fairly regular bedtime and time that he or she awakens?

Scoring: For a score of "3" or less (i.e., less than every night), refer to Module 2: Good Sleep Hygiene for intervention suggestions on creating sleep schedules.

2. Does the child have a bedtime routine that is the same each evening?

Scoring: For a score of "3" or less (i.e., less than every night), refer to Module 2: Good Sleep Hygiene for intervention suggestions on establishing bedtime routines.

3. Does the child work or play in bed often right up to the time he or she goes to bed?

Scoring: For a score of "2" or more (i.e., one or more times per week), refer to Module 2: Good Sleep Hygiene for intervention suggestions around establishing stimulus control.

4. Does the child sleep poorly in his or her own bed, but better away from it?

Scoring: If the parents respond with a "Yes," refer to Module 2: Good Sleep Hygiene for intervention suggestions around establishing stimulus control.

5. Does the child consume caffeine in any form?

Scoring: For a score of "2" or more (i.e., one or more times per week), refer to Module 2: Good Sleep Hygiene for intervention suggestions on identifying and consuming caffeine.

6. Does the child engage in vigorous activity in the hours before bedtime?

Scoring: For a score of "2" or more (i.e., one or more times per week), refer to Module 2: Good Sleep Hygiene for intervention suggestions on the appropriate use of exercise.

Bedtime and Night Waking Questions

7. Does the child resist going to bed?

Scoring: For a score of "2" or more (i.e., one or more times per week), refer to Module 3: Bedtime for intervention suggestions.

8. Does the child take more than an hour to fall asleep but does not resist?

Scoring: For a score of "2" or more (i.e., one or more times per week), refer to Module 3: Bedtime for intervention suggestions, especially for "sleep restriction."

9. Does the child awaken during the night but remain quiet and in bed?

Scoring: For a score of "2" or more (i.e., one or more times per week), refer to Module 4: Night Waking for intervention suggestions, especially for "sleep restriction" or "scheduled awakening."

10. Does the child awaken during the night and is he or she disruptive (e.g., tantrums, oppositional)?

Scoring: For a score of "2" or more (i.e., one or more times per week), refer to Module 4: Night Waking for intervention suggestions.

Sleepiness Questions

11. Does the child take naps during the day?

Scoring: For a score of "2" or more (i.e., one or more times per week) and *bedtime* is a problem, refer to Module 3: Bedtime for intervention suggestions. If the parents respond with a score of "2" or more (i.e., one or more times per week) and *night waking* is a problem, refer to Module 4: Night Waking for intervention suggestions.

12. Does the child often feel exhausted during the day because of lack of sleep?

Scoring: For a score of "2" or more (i.e., one or more times per week) and *bedtime* is a problem, refer to Module 3: Bedtime for intervention suggestions. If the parents respond with a score of "2" or more (i.e., one or more times per week) and *night waking* is a problem, refer to Module 4: Night Waking for intervention suggestions. If the parents respond with a score of "2" or more (i.e., one or more times per week) and *neither* bedtime nor night waking is a problem, refer to Module 7: Other Sleep-Related Issues for guidance and intervention suggestions.

13. Has the child ever had an accident or near accident because of sleepiness from not being able to sleep the night before?

Scoring: If the parents respond with a "Yes" and *bedtime* is a problem, refer to Module 3: Bedtime for intervention suggestions. If the parents respond with a "Yes" and *night waking* is a problem, refer to Module 4: Night Waking for intervention suggestions. If the parents respond with a "Yes" and *neither* bedtime nor night waking is a problem, refer to Module 7: Other Sleep-Related Issues for guidance and intervention suggestions.

Medication Use Questions

14. Does the child ever use prescription drugs or over-the-counter medications to help him or her sleep?

Scoring: For a score of "2" or more (i.e., one or more times per week), you will need to assess parents' willingness to titrate the child off of the medication. The family's physician or child's pediatrician needs to be involved in this decision and plan. One important factor about using medications to sleep is that it is not usually recommended to use them for more than a few weeks. In most cases, sleep professionals view medication as a temporary measure to be used until a more formal plan is designed.

15. Has the child found that sleep medication doesn't work as well as it did when he or she first started taking it?

Scoring: If the parents respond with a "Yes," you will need to assess their willingness to titrate the child off of the medication. The family's physician or child's pediatrician needs to be involved in this decision and plan. When used for too long, children (and adults) begin to tolerate sleep medication so that they need more of it to be effective.

16. If taking sleep medication, does the child find that he or she can't sleep on nights without it?

Scoring: If the parents respond with a "Yes," you will need to assess their willingness to titrate the child off of the medication. The family's physician or child's pediatrician needs to be involved in this decision and plan. Sometimes medication has a negative effect on sleep when it is stopped, a phenomenon known as rebound insomnia, which serves to disrupt sleep after it is no longer used.

Sleep Schedule Questions

17. Does the child fall asleep early in the evening and awaken too early in the morning?

18. Does the child have difficulty falling asleep until a very late hour and difficulty awakening early in the morning?

Scoring: For a score of "2" or more (i.e., one or more times per week) on either of these questions and *bedtime* is a problem, refer to Module 3: Bedtime for intervention suggestions. For a score of "2" or more (i.e., one or more times per week) and *night waking* is a problem, refer to Module 4: Night Waking for intervention suggestions. For a score of "2" or more (i.e., one or more times per week) and *neither* bedtime nor night waking is a problem, refer to Module 7: Other Sleep-Related Issues for guidance and intervention suggestions.

Nightmare Questions

19. Does the child wake up in the middle of the night upset?

Scoring: For a score of "2" or more (i.e., one or more times per week), or a "1" but the parents are very concerned, further information is needed. It is important to differentiate nightmares—which are disturbing dreams—from sleep terrors. If the child is waking up after these episodes and can calm down and be comforted after such a dream, refer to Module 5: Nightmare and Sleep Terrors for intervention suggestions for nightmares. If the child is *not* waking up and cannot be calmed down and comforted, refer to Module 5 for intervention suggestions for sleep terrors.

20. Is the child relatively easy to comfort during these episodes?

Scoring: If the parents respond with a "Yes," refer to Module 5: Nightmare and Sleep Terrors for intervention suggestions for nightmares. If the parents respond with a "No," refer to Module 5 for intervention suggestions for sleep terrors.

Sleep Terror Questions

21. Does the child have episodes during sleep where he or she screams loudly for several minutes but is not fully awake?

Scoring: For a score of "2" or more (i.e., one or more times per week), or a "1" but the parents are very concerned, refer to Module 5: Nightmare and Sleep Terrors for intervention suggestions for sleep terrors.

22. Is the child difficult to comfort during these episodes?

Scoring: If the parents respond with a "Yes," refer to Module 5: Nightmare and Sleep Terrors for intervention suggestions for sleep terrors.

Hypersomnia and Narcolepsy Questions

23. Does the child experience sleep attacks (falling asleep almost immediately and without warning) during the day?

Scoring: For a score of "1" or more, refer to Module 7: Other Sleep-Related Issues for more information on narcolepsy or hypersomnia. It is recommended that the child be evaluated by a physician or a sleep specialist if any of these problems is suspected.

24. Does the child experience excessive daytime sleepiness that is not due to an inadequate amount of sleep?

Scoring: For a score of "1" or more, refer to Module 7: Other Sleep-Related Issues for more information on hypersomnia, limb movement disorders, and breathing-related disorders. If the child seems tired during the day or if frequent night waking is a problem and hypersomnia, limb movement disorders, and/or breathing-related disorders are a suspected cause, the child should be evaluated by a physician or a sleep specialist.

Breathing-Related Questions

25. Does the child snore when asleep?

Scoring: For a score of "2" or more (i.e., one or more times per week), refer to Module 7: Other Sleep-Related Issues for more information on breathing problems. If the child seems tired during the day or if frequent night waking is a problem and breathing problems are a suspected cause, the child should be evaluated by a physician or a sleep specialist.

26. Does the child sometimes stop breathing for a few seconds during sleep?

Scoring: For a score of "1" or more (i.e., less than once per week but more than never), refer to Module 7: Other Sleep-Related Issues for more information on breathing problems. If the child seems tired during the day or if frequent night waking is a problem and breathing problems are a suspected cause, the child should be evaluated by a physician or a sleep specialist.

27. Does the child have trouble breathing?

Scoring: For a score of "1" or more (i.e., less than once per week but more than never), refer to Module 7: Other Sleep-Related Issues for more information on breathing problems. If the child seems tired during the day or if frequent night waking is a problem and breathing problems are a suspected cause, the child should be evaluated by a physician or a sleep specialist.

28. Is the child overweight?

Scoring: If the parents respond with a "Yes," refer to Module 7: Other Sleep-Related Issues for more information on potential breathing problems. If the child seems tired during the day or if frequent night waking is a problem and breathing problems are a suspected cause, the child should be evaluated by a physician or a sleep specialist.

Sleepwalking and Sleeptalking Questions

29. Has the child often walked when asleep?

30. Does the child talk while asleep?

Scoring: For a score of "2" or more (i.e., one or more times per week) on either of these questions, refer to Module 7: Other Sleep-Related Issues for information and intervention suggestions for sleepwalking and related problems.

Limb Movement and Rhythmic Movement Questions

31. Are the child's sheets and blankets in extreme disarray in the morning when he or she wakes up?

Scoring: For a score of "2" or more (i.e., one or more times per week), refer to Module 7: Other Sleep-Related Issues for more information on limb movement problems. If the child seems tired during the day or if frequent night waking is a problem and limb movements are a suspected cause, the child should be evaluated by a physician or a sleep specialist.

32. Does the child wake up at night because of kicking legs?

Scoring: As with question #31, a score of "2" or more (i.e., one or more times per week) may suggest that periodic limb movements are interfering with sleep. If the child seems tired during the day or if frequent night waking is a problem and limb movements are a suspected cause, the child should be evaluated by a physician or a sleep specialist.

33. While lying down, does the child ever experience unpleasant sensations in the legs?

Scoring: If the parents respond with a "Yes," this may be a sign that the child suffers from restless legs syndrome, which can cause insomnia in some people. A physician or a sleep specialist should evaluate the child.

34. Does the child rock back and forth or bang a body part (e.g., head) to fall asleep?

Scoring: For a score of "2" or more (i.e., one or more times per week), or a "1" but the parents are very concerned, refer to Module 7: Other Sleep-

Related Issues for more information. These types of rhythmic movements are common, even in some adults. When they begin to cause injury, as with some children who bang their heads, intervention is recommended.

Bedwetting Questions

35. Does the child wet the bed?

Scoring: If the parents respond with a score of "2" or more (i.e., one or more times per week) or a "1" but are very concerned, refer to Module 6: Bedwetting for information and intervention suggestions. Up until the age of about 5 years, bedwetting is not considered a problem. However, after that age, children should be sleeping through the night without accidents.

Teeth Grinding Questions

36. Does the child grind his or her teeth at night?

Scoring: For a score of "2" or more (i.e., one or more times per week), refer to Module 7: Other Sleep-Related Issues for more information on teeth grinding. It is recommended that the child be evaluated by a pediatrician.

Anxiety and Depression Questions

37. Does the child sleep well when it doesn't matter, such as on weekends, but sleeps poorly when he or she "must" sleep well, such as when a busy day at school is ahead?

38. Does the child often have feelings of apprehension, anxiety, or dread when he or she is getting ready for bed?

39. Does the child worry in bed?

40. Does the child often have depressing thoughts, or do tomorrow's worries or plans buzz through his or her mind when he or she wants to go to sleep?

41. Does the child have feelings of frustration when he or she can't sleep?

42. Has the child experienced a relatively recent change in eating habits?

Scoring: For a response of "Yes" or a score of "2" or more (i.e., one or more times per week) to any of the questions in this section, refer to Module 7: Other Sleep-Related Issues for information and intervention suggestions for anxiety and depression.

Daytime Behavior Problem Questions

43. Does the child have behavior problems at times other than bedtime or upon awakening?

This question is included because 1) getting a handle on daytime behavior problems can often help with bedtime problems and, 2) daytime behavior problems and sleep problems are often related, and it is important to consider them together.

Other Causes

44. When did the child's primary difficulty with sleep begin?

Answers here may provide additional information about the potential causes of disrupted sleep (e.g., problems at school).

45. What was happening in the child's life at that time, or a few months before?

Again, answers here may provide additional information about the potential causes of disrupted sleep (e.g., illness or vacations that preceded the current problems).

46. Is the child under a physician's care for any medical condition?

It is important to know if medical conditions or the treatments for these problems (e.g., medications) are contributing to the child's sleep difficulties.

Parents should keep a Sleep Diary of their child's sleep patterns for 2 weeks. Ask parents to complete the Sleep Diary form each day and bring it to the next session. This tool measures basic information such as the time the child was put in bed and approximately what time the child fell asleep. This will give you an idea about how long the child takes to fall asleep each night.

The Sleep Diary also indicates if and how many times the child may have awakened during the night. If there were any awakenings, you should ask the parent to describe them. This information reveals how much the child's sleep is disrupted, and the kind of problems the parents face. If night waking or bedtime are significant problems, have the parents also complete a Behavior Log form as described next.

Finally, information about the time the child wakes up each morning and naps tells you about any schedule problems (for example, the child wakes up too early), and the way sleep is or is not spread out during the day. The total amount of sleep time can be calculated by adding up the number of shaded boxes.

The corresponding workbook chapter includes a blank copy of both the Sleep Diary and the Behavior Log. Additional blank forms are provided in appendices to the workbook—you may photocopy extra forms as needed.

Sample Sleep Diary

See figure 2.1 for an example of a Sleep Diary that describes 1 week of sleep data for Ethan, a 5-year-old boy. Ethan's parents and teacher were concerned because he was tired during the day, and he would be up most of the early evening. You can see from his Sleep Diary several sleep habits that may have had a negative influence on his sleep. First, notice that Ethan has no set bedtime, sometimes being put in bed as early as 10:00 P.M., and sometimes as late as 1:00 A.M. Many children seem to need a stable bedtime and bedtime routine, and without it, they may have difficulty falling asleep. Module 2: Good Sleep Hygiene describes how to establish a routine for a child like Ethan.

SLEEP DIARY for _Ethan_

Instructions: Shade in the times when the child is asleep. Mark bedtime with a down arrow and time awake with an up arrow.

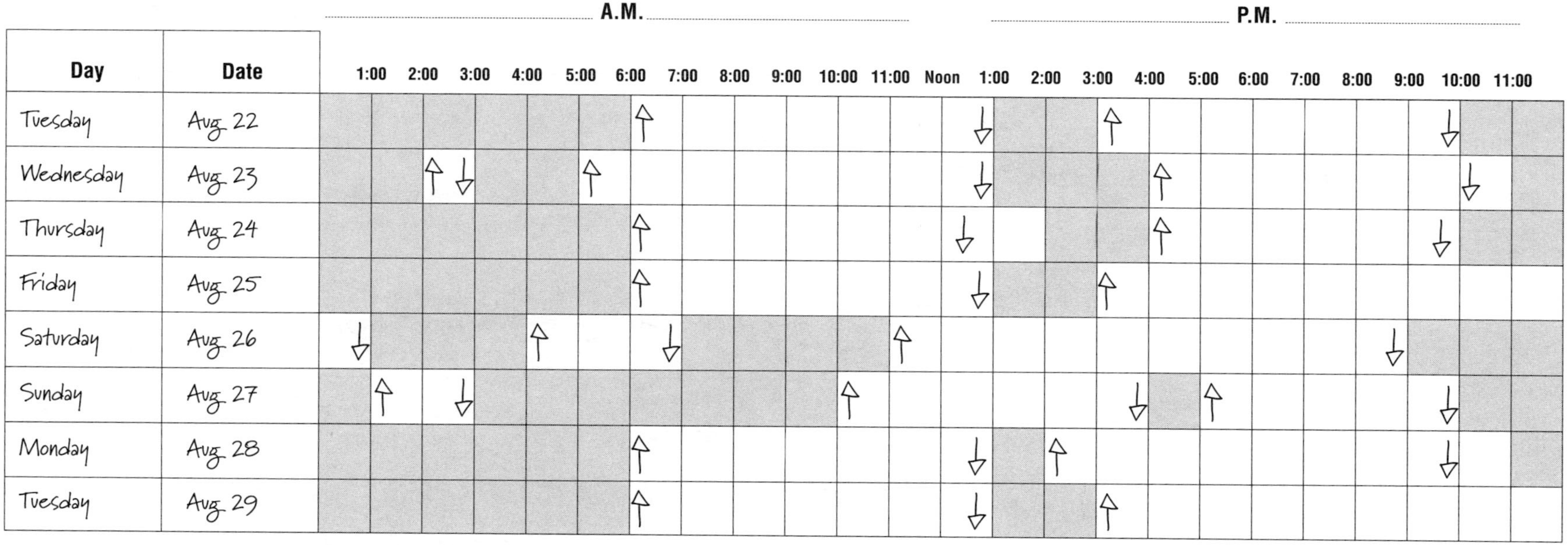

Figure 2.1.

Example of Completed Sleep Diary for Ethan

BEHAVIOR LOG for _____Emma_____

Date	Time	Behavior at Bedtime	Your Response	Behavior During Awakenings	Your Response
3/19	9:15	Crying, throwing toys	Told her to stop, let her fall asleep on the couch		
3/20	9:30	Crying, screaming	Let her fall asleep in my lap		
3/20	12:30			Crying "Mommy!"	Let her come into our bed
3/21	9:15	Whining	Let her watch TV until she fell asleep in the TV room		

Figure 2.2

Example of Completed Behavior Log for Emma

The next thing you notice from Ethan's Sleep Diary is that he takes naps during the day. Because he is getting only about 6 to 7 hours of sleep each night during the week, it is not surprising that he is tired during the day and that he would nap when he can to "catch up" on missed sleep. Unfortunately, these naps may contribute to his inability to fall asleep at night. Notice, too, that he napped less over the weekend when he was allowed to sleep as late as he wanted. Based on this information about his sleep, we designed a new sleep schedule for Ethan that helped him fall asleep in the evening and not nap at school.

Sample Behavior Log

If night waking or bedtime are issues, parents record their child's behavior at bedtime and during the night on a Behavior Log, as well as keep a Sleep Diary. This helps determine the extent and nature of behavior problems associated with sleep. The example in Figure 2.2 comes from just 3 nights of recording for one 3-year-old girl—Emma. Note that Emma's mother tends to "give in" to her resistance at bedtime (by letting her fall asleep outside of her bedroom), and allows her to sleep in her parent's bed after awaking at night. Not only is this a problem for Emma because she is not learning to fall asleep in her bed, but it also indicates that her mother will have a hard time following through with an intervention. You will further assess family reluctance through the use of the Sleep Intervention Questionnaire (SIQ) in Session 2.

Homework

- ✎ Have parents complete the Sleep Diary on a daily basis.
- ✎ Have parents complete the Behavior Log as needed.
- ✎ Assign reading of Chapters 1–3 of the workbook.

Second Session

Data Analysis and Treatment Planning

(Corresponds to chapter 2 of the workbook)

Materials Needed

- Completed Albany Sleep Problems Scale (ASPS)
- Partially completed Sleep Diary
- Partially completed Behavior Log
- Sleep Intervention Questionnaire (SIQ)

Outline

- Set agenda
- Identify nature of sleep problems using results from ASPS
- Review parent's data from Sleep Diary
- Review parent's data from Behavior Log
- Provide information about sleep schedules and habits
- Administer the Sleep Intervention Questionnaire (SIQ)
- Discuss the results of the SIQ
- Discuss next steps
- Assign homework

Setting the Agenda

Provide the family with an overview of the session as well as the expectations for the homework. You should encourage their continued patience and remind them that there are a number of different approaches that can be used to successfully improve their child's sleep.

Nature of Sleep Problems

Use the responses from the ASPS to summarize the different types of sleep problems and those that seem to be applicable to the child. Where appropriate—for example, when breathing-related and limb movement problems are suspected—refer parents to their pediatrician or family physician for follow-up.

Review of Sleep Diary

If the family kept good records, make sure to reinforce this effort. If they did not follow through with record-keeping, try to get them to recall the previous week's episodes as best as they can. Lack of data-keeping can be the result of a busy week, or it can be a sign that the family may not be able to carry out sleep interventions. This concern will be assessed later in the session when you administer the Sleep Intervention Questionnaire.

Use the parent's partially completed Sleep Diary to calculate how long, on average, the child sleeps each day (combining both nighttime and daytime sleeping). This average will be used to assess variations in the child's sleep. It may also be used to plan for sleep restriction if part of the intervention. Also note how often the child sleeps during the day (naps) and the presence of a consistent time to awaken and bedtime. Napping may be interfering with nighttime sleep and may be a target for intervention. The lack of a consistent bedtime and/or time to awaken will also be a target for intervention.

Review of Behavior Log

Review the parent's partially completed Behavior Log to assess how disruptive the child is around sleep. This is also a time to ask how disruptive the child's behavior is to others (e.g., siblings, neighbors). Crisis intervention techniques may be necessary so that families have a consistent way to handle disturbances. Any number of typical behavioral approaches can be used here as long as:

- The child is protected from harm

- The family limits how much attention is given to the disruptive behavior (e.g., limiting long discussions about how important it is to behave or to get a good night's sleep)

- Each parent agrees to the same approach

We have found that as long as these guidelines are met, the specific crisis intervention technique used by parents can be modified considerably. Some parents use timers to give them a realistic picture of just how long their child is crying—which seems endless—and they encourage each other's patience in waiting it out. Other parents feel very uncomfortable ignoring misbehavior, so we encourage them to intervene minimally—without talking—in order to be sure everything is safe. Serious behavior problems require more specific behavioral interventions.

Sleep Schedules and Habits

Almost 75% of sleep problems can be resolved with proper sleep hygiene. Briefly review the importance of sleep schedules—a regular time to go to bed and a regular time to wake up—especially on weekends. Also review the major sleep hygiene issues (e.g., bedtime routines, caffeine use, diet, exercise, etc.). If any of these issues are problematic, they will be covered in the next session (Module 2: Good Sleep Hygiene).

Our experience suggests that a major barrier to treatment success on the part of primary caregivers is attitudinal. Specifically, we find that many families experience significant guilt when pressed to intervene with their child's sleep problems. Although many recognize the need for their child to fall asleep or go back to sleep alone, the parents' emotional reaction to crying can be sufficient to interfere with an intervention plan. To assess the extent to which you may experience this reluctance from a family, administer the Sleep Intervention Questionnaire (SIQ). The SIQ assists with treatment design. Once the nature of the sleep problem is identified, the SIQ helps narrow the types of intervention choices suitable for the family. The questions from the SIQ and information on scoring follow. A blank copy of the SIQ can be found in an appendix to this manual.

Disruption Tolerance

1. Does your child misbehave at bedtime or when waking up at night in a way that is too serious or upsetting to ignore?

2. Would it be difficult or impossible for you to listen to your child being upset for long periods of time (more than a few minutes)?

3. Do you find it too difficult to put your child back in bed once he or she gets up?

Scoring: If the parents answer "Yes" to one or more of these questions, they may not be good candidates for using *graduated extinction* as an intervention for their child's sleep problems.

Schedule Tolerance

4. Are you, or another member of your family, willing to stay up later at night to put a sleep plan into action?

5. Are you, or another member of your family, willing to get up earlier in the morning to put a sleep plan into action?

Scoring: If the parents answer "No" to one or more of these questions, they may not be good candidates for *scheduled awakenings* or *sleep restriction* as interventions for their child's sleep problems.

Attitudinal Barriers

6. Do you feel emotionally unable to deal directly with your child's sleep problem?

7. Do you feel guilty making your child go to bed (or go back to bed) when he or she does not want to?

8. Do you think it would be emotionally damaging to your child if you tried to change the way he or she slept?

Scoring: If the parents answer "Yes" to one or more of these questions, they may need cognitive-behavioral intervention to explore their attitudes about their ability or their child's ability to improve sleep.

Results of the SIQ

Go over the answers to the questionnaire with the parents, getting validation on issues related to their reluctance to intervene with their child. Especially note discrepancies between parents. Emphasize that you will be working together to select an intervention that they can adhere to. You should revisit this assessment in each intervention section to aid treatment adherence.

Next Steps

Based on previous findings from the ASPS and the data collected by the parents on the Sleep Diary and Behavior Log, discuss how to prioritize sleep problems if there are multiple needs. We have data to suggest that if both bedtime and night waking are problems, it is best to first intervene with bedtime problems (Mindell & Durand, 1993). Typically, a resolution to bedtime problems is accompanied by a resolution to night waking.

Use the Decision-Tree for Sleep Interventions (Figure 2.3) at the end of this chapter to help you select the next module for treatment.

Homework

✎ Encourage parents to continue completing the Sleep Diary and, if needed, the Behavior Log.

✎ Assign appropriate readings in the workbook, depending on the next module.

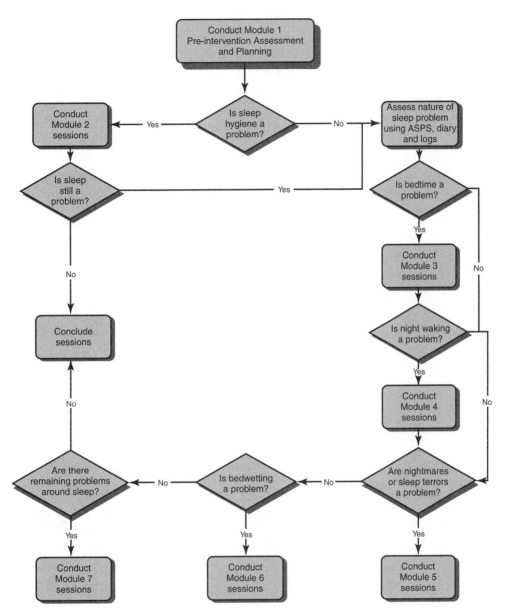

Figure 2.3.

Decision-Tree for Sleep Interventions

Module 2
Good Sleep Hygiene

Improving Sleep Hygiene

(Corresponds to chapter 3 of the workbook)

Materials Needed

- Completed Albany Sleep Problems Scale (ASPS)
- Completed Sleep Intervention Questionnaire (SIQ)
- Completed Sleep Diary
- Completed Behavior Log

Outline

- Set agenda
- Review homework
- Discuss importance of good sleep habits
- Discuss age-related sleep needs
- Identify sleep hygiene problems and suggest changes
- Help family prioritize sleep hygiene issues
- Assign homework

Setting the Agenda

Provide the family with an overview of the session as well as the expectations for the homework. Encourage their continued patience and remind them that there are a number of different approaches that can be used to successfully improve their child's sleep.

Homework Review

Review the completed Sleep Diary and Behavior Log for the past week. Discuss any changes in the child's sleep.

Importance of Good Sleep Habits

Emphasize to the parents that a number of habits can affect sleep:

- What and when we eat and drink

- When we exercise

- Bedroom temperature

- Any noise

- What we do in bed (e.g., watching TV, playing games)

Highlight that everyday activities that we tend to take for granted can impact on how well we fall to sleep and if we stay asleep. This is especially true for children with sleep problems. Parents need to provide more structure surrounding sleep hygiene for children who have any difficulty sleeping.

Age-Related Sleep Needs

Emphasize that the average amount of sleep a child needs diminishes as the child grows older. By 6 months, all children should be able to sleep through the night without being fed and fall asleep on their own. Table 3.1 can be used to estimate the average sleep need for a child of a certain age.

Sleep needs differ by age but also by individual child. If a child is sleeping somewhat less than average but functions well during the day and

Table 3.1 Sleep Needs by Age

Age	Average Sleep Needs (approximate)
6 months–2 years	13 hours
2–3 years	12 hours
3–5 years	11 hours
5–9 years	10.5 hours (no longer taking naps)
9–13 years	10 hours
13–18 years	8.5 hours

does not seem tired, she may be getting sufficient sleep. On the other hand, if a child is getting the average amount of sleep for her age and is still tired, the child may require more sleep.

Sleep Hygiene Problems and Changes

Use the responses from the ASPS and any follow-up discussion to identify potentially problematic sleep hygiene issues and suggest changes. The corresponding workbook chapter also includes a sleep habits checklist that relates to the following questions:

1. **Does the child have a fairly regular bedtime and time when she awakens?**

    No → Instruct the family to:
    - Estimate the approximate number of hours of sleep for the goal (based on child's sleep needs)
    - Determine a good wake time that fits with the family's and the child's schedule
    - Move backwards from the desired wake time the number of optimal sleep hours to find the best bedtime (e.g., 7 A.M. minus 10 hours = 9 P.M. bedtime)
    - Try to stay with this sleep-wake schedule each day—even on weekends

2. **Does the child have a bedtime routine that is the same each evening?**

   No → Instruct the family to:
   - Make the last 30 minutes before bedtime a regular routine
   - Include calming activities such as dressing for sleep, washing, and reading
   - Keep the order and timing of the activities about the same each night
   - Do not include activities that could cause conflict (e.g., picking out clothes for school, organizing homework)
   - Avoid television watching during this time, which can interfere with sleep
   - Avoid extending the time for the bedtime routine (i.e., do not allow bedtime activities to take up more time than allotted)

3. **Does the child work or play in bed, often right up to the time when she goes to bed?**

   Yes → Instruct the family to:
   - Avoid any activity in bed other than sleeping or routines leading up to sleeping

4. **Does the child sleep poorly in her own bed, but better away from it?**

   Yes → Instruct the family to:
   - Avoid any activity in bed other than sleeping or routines leading up to sleeping
   - Follow bedtime routines and the other good sleep habits

5. **Does the child consume caffeine in any form?**

   Yes → Instruct the family to:
   - Reduce the amount of caffeine used by the child during the day (including soda, chocolate, nonprescription drugs)
   - Eliminate all intake of caffeine at least 6 hours before bedtime

6. **Does the child engage in vigorous activity in the hours before bedtime?**

   Yes → Instruct the family to:
   - Try to establish a daily exercise regime for the child

- Consult with a physician before starting any new exercise programs
- Encourage the child to engage in aerobic exercise 4–6 hours before bedtime
- Discourage the child from exercising or engaging in vigorous activity right before bedtime
- If appropriate, look for ways to decrease boredom and increase activity throughout the day

7. **Does the child take more than an hour to fall asleep but does not resist, or does the child awaken at night but remains quiet and in bed?**

Yes → Instruct the family to:
- Consider a later bedtime
- Encourage the child to get out of bed if she cannot fall asleep within 15 minutes
- Have the child sit somewhere else in the room and read or engage in some other quiet activity until she is tired, then go back to bed and try to fall asleep again
- Consider sleep restriction for bedtime (Module 3) or night waking (Module 4) problems

8. **Does the child's diet encourage good sleeping?**

No → Instruct the family to:
- Consider milk before bedtime (but not so much that it leads to toileting problems)
- Consider low-fat foods at dinner and prior to bedtime to reduce stomach distress

9. **Does the child's bedroom discourage sleep because of noise, lights, or temperature?**

Yes → Instruct the family to:
- Keep the household relatively quiet at bedtime if noise can be heard in the bedroom
- Minimize light in the bedroom, using a nightlight if necessary
- Keep the room temperature comfortable (not too hot or cold)

Prioritizing Sleep Hygiene Issues

Help the family select from the sleep hygiene issues if multiple concerns are raised. Simple changes (for example, reducing caffeine use) can occur immediately. Bedtime routines and set times for sleeping are usually recommended as the most important areas for change if they are problematic, but can also be difficult to establish. Weekend sleep patterns ("sleeping in") are usually contentious for both the parents and the child and should be negotiated (e.g., not waking the child up at 7:00 A.M. as on a school day, but not letting her sleep until noon).

The corresponding workbook chapter includes a table summarizing many of the dos and don'ts of good sleep hygiene. Refer parents to the strategies listed as needed.

Homework

✎ Have parents begin to implement good sleep habits as discussed during the session and continue to complete a Sleep Diary on a daily basis.

✎ If parents are to establish a bedtime routine, they should record the results using a Sleep Diary and Behavior Log.

✎ Assign review of Chapter 3 of the workbook.

Follow-Up Sessions | *Sleep Hygiene*

(Corresponds to chapter 3 of the workbook)

Materials Needed

- Completed Albany Sleep Problems Scale (ASPS)

- Completed Sleep Intervention Questionnaire (SIQ)

- Completed Sleep Diary

- Completed Behavior Log

Outline

- Set agenda

- Discuss family's progress since last session

- Discuss necessary modifications

- Address remaining sleep hygiene issues

- Assign homework

Setting the Agenda

Provide the family with an overview of the session as well as the expectations for the homework. If sleep is still a problem, encourage their continued patience and remind them that there are a number of different approaches that can be used to successfully improve their child's sleep.

Depending on the child's progress, you may spend more than one session on sleep hygiene.

Review of Progress

Discuss the child's progress as a result of the family implementing sleep hygiene changes. It is important at this time to encourage the accurate reporting of changes the family did or did not complete. Less than 100% compliance (e.g., "we let her have a soda with dinner Tuesday night because we were out") is to be expected. The goal is continual progress, and any interruptions can be treated as assessments (e.g., "Did she have more trouble falling asleep on Tuesday after having caffeine?").

Modifications

If needed, some leeway is permissible in the sleep hygiene interventions. Modification of strategies is often possible without seriously compromising effectiveness. Priority at this point should be given to encouraging families to make incremental progress. This is particularly important for bedtime routines as well as sleep and wake times.

Often, the most difficult obstacle is getting parents to adhere to bedtimes and wake times during the weekend. When this is a problem, we typically negotiate a modified weekend sleep-wake schedule. For example, instead of waking the child at the typical school time (e.g., 6:30 A.M.), we look for time halfway between that time and the time the child would typically awaken on her own if allowed to "sleep in" (e.g., 11:30 A.M.). Similarly, a modified weekend bedtime is allowable. We usually encourage that bedtime on the weekend be no later than one hour past the typical bedtime.

Remaining Sleep Hygiene Issues

If the family wasn't able to implement all the recommendations or there are remaining sleep hygiene issues, outline recommendations for the coming weeks.

If sleep has improved, encourage continued monitoring for at least several weeks to assess effectiveness. If there is no measurable progress after 2 to 3 weeks of implementing sleep hygiene strategies, use the decision tree in Module 1 to select the direction of the next sessions.

Homework

✎ If sleep hygiene changes are producing positive changes in sleep, have parents continue monitoring with the Sleep Diary and, if needed, Behavior Log.

✎ If sleep hygiene changes are not producing adequate changes or parents are unable to make changes, prepare them to go to the next appropriate module and assign readings and homework.

Module 3
Bedtime

First Session

Improving Bedtime

(Corresponds to chapter 4 of the workbook)

Materials Needed

- Completed Albany Sleep Problems Scale (ASPS)
- Completed Sleep Intervention Questionnaire (SIQ)
- Completed Sleep Diary
- Completed Behavior Log

Outline

- Set agenda
- Review homework
- Describe intervention options for improving bedtime
- Select the appropriate intervention for the family
- Deal with family resistance, if necessary
- Present steps for graduated extinction (if selected intervention)
- Present steps for sleep restriction (if selected intervention)
- Assign homework

Setting the Agenda

Provide the family with an overview of the session as well as the expectations for the homework. Encourage their continued patience and remind them that there are a number of different approaches that can be used to successfully improve bedtime.

Homework Review

Review the completed Sleep Diary and Behavior Log for the past week. Discuss any progress the child has made. If sleep hygiene habits have been changed, determine whether these are having any effect.

Intervention Options

If modifying sleep hygiene habits (especially bedtime routines and sleep-wake schedule) has not been successful in improving bedtime behavior, the next step is to try one of two interventions for bedtime problems: graduated extinction and sleep restriction. The selection between these two approaches is based primarily on which one fits best with the family. Begin with a general discussion of the two interventions, including their pros and cons.

Graduated Extinction

Graduated extinction involves spending increasingly longer amounts of time ignoring the cries and protests of a child at bedtime. The goal of this treatment is to fade the amount of time the parents attend to the child around bedtime while giving them the opportunity to check on their child. The mechanism of change appears to involve forcing the child to learn to fall asleep on his own.

Sleep Restriction

Sleep restriction involves reducing the amount of time the child sleeps and then gradually increasing the time to a healthy amount. This can involve moving bedtime later in the evening or waking the child up earlier

Table 4.1 Pros and Cons of Graduated Extinction and Sleep Restriction

	Pros	Cons
Graduated Extinction	+ Begins during regular bedtime	− Long bouts of crying/tantrums
	+ Allows for checking on the child	− Can be a temporary increase in crying/tantrums
		− Not useful for nondisruptive sleep-initiation problems
Sleep Restriction	+ Avoids most crying/tantrums	− Requires family member to stay up later with the child
	+ Can be used for nondisruptive sleep-initiation problems	− Can be difficult to keep child awake for new bedtime

in the morning. The goal of this treatment is to adjust the sleep amount such that it causes drowsiness and decreases the likelihood of bedtime disturbances. The mechanism of change appears to be creating the conditions (sleep deprivation) that make it easier for the child to practice falling asleep without parents present.

Pros and Cons

Use Table 4.1 to help the family consider the advantages and disadvantages of each approach.

Intervention Selection

After describing the interventions, discuss concerns parents may have with either approach. Use their responses to the Sleep Intervention Questionnaire (SIQ) to identify potential obstacles. A review of SIQ categories follows.

Disruption Tolerance

If parents responded "Yes" to one or more of the following questions on the SIQ, then they may not be good candidates for graduated extinction.

1. Does your child misbehave at bedtime or when waking up at night in a way that is too serious or upsetting to ignore?

2. Would it be difficult or impossible for you to listen to your child being upset for long periods of time (more than a few minutes)?

3. Do you find it too difficult to put your child back in bed once he gets up?

Schedule Tolerance

If parents responded "No" to one or more of the following questions on the SIQ, then you need to discuss which would be the least disruptive to the family—graduated extinction or sleep restriction.

4. Are you, or another member of your family, willing to stay up later at night to put a sleep plan into action?

5. Are you, or another member of your family, willing to get up earlier in the morning to put a sleep plan into action?

Attitudinal Barriers

A response of "Yes" to one of the following questions on the SIQ may require further intervention with the family to prepare them for any intervention (see the next section on dealing with family resistance).

6. Do you feel emotionally unable to deal directly with your child's sleep problem?

7. Do you feel guilty making your child go to bed (or go back to bed) when he does not want to?

8. Do you think it would be emotionally damaging to your child if you tried to change the way he slept?

Dealing with Family Resistance

Some families require brief cognitive-behavioral intervention to deal with feelings of guilt surrounding their child's sleep problems. You will need to:

1. Assess the ability of parents to intervene at all with their child.

2. Assign, if necessary, just one parent to intervene if the other cannot.

3. Challenge self-talk that interferes with successful intervention (e.g., "My child will be angry with me if I make him sleep alone," or "I am a bad parent if my child is upset at bedtime.").

4. Determine if more extensive intervention is necessary prior to implementing a sleep plan.

Steps for Graduated Extinction

If graduated extinction is selected as the treatment of choice, follow these steps:

1. Remind the family to maintain a regular bedtime routine.

2. Set an agreed upon bedtime that will not change over the course of the intervention.

3. Negotiate the amount of time for the parents to wait before going in to check on their child. A typical time would be between 3–5 minutes the first night.

4. Pick the night to begin the plan, assuming no one will have a good night's sleep that evening—most families begin on a Friday night.

5. On the first night have the parents follow the bedtime routine, put the child to bed at the regular bedtime, leave the room, and then wait the agreed upon time (e.g., 3 minutes) before checking on the child.

6. If after waiting the full amount of time the child is still crying, parents can go into the room, tell him to go to bed, then leave.

They should not pick up the child, give him food or a drink, or engage in extensive conversation.

7. Have parents wait the same amount of time (e.g., 3 minutes) before going back into the room each time. They should continue the pattern until the child is asleep or until they feel comfortable waiting longer.

8. On each subsequent night, have parents extend the time between visits by 2 or 3 minutes. They should continue the same procedure as in step 6 when returning to the child's room.

Steps for Sleep Restriction

If sleep restriction is selected as the treatment of choice, follow these steps:

1. Select a bedtime when the child is likely to fall asleep with little difficulty and within about 15 minutes. To determine this bedtime, use the Sleep Diary to find a time when the child falls asleep if left alone (e.g., 1 A.M.), then add 30 minutes to this time (e.g, new bedtime = 1:30 A.M.).

2. If the child falls asleep within 15 minutes of being put to bed at this new bedtime and without resistance for 2 successive nights, move the bedtime back by 15 minutes (e.g., from 1:30 A.M. to 1:15 A.M.).

3. Have parents keep the child awake before the new bedtime, even if he seems to want to fall asleep.

4. If the child does not fall asleep within about 15 minutes after being put to bed, parents should have him leave the bedroom and extend the bedtime for one more hour.

5. Have parents continue to move the bedtime back (e.g., from 1:15 A.M. to 1:00 A.M.) until the desired bedtime is reached.

6. Have parents maintain a regular time to awaken the child and warn them to resist letting the child "sleep in."

Homework

✎ Have parents implement the selected intervention as discussed during the session.

✎ Have parents continue to complete the Sleep Diary on a daily basis.

✎ Have parents continue to complete the Behavior Log on a daily basis.

✎ Assign review of Chapter 4 of the workbook.

Follow-Up Sessions

Bedtime Intervention

(Corresponds to chapter 4 of the workbook)

Materials Needed

- Completed Albany Sleep Problems Scale (ASPS)
- Completed Sleep Intervention Questionnaire (SIQ)
- Completed Sleep Diary
- Completed Behavior Log

Outline

- Set agenda
- Discuss family's progress since last session
- Discuss necessary modifications
- Address remaining bedtime issues
- Assign homework

Setting the Agenda

Provide the family with an overview of the session as well as the expectations for the homework. If bedtime is still a problem, encourage their continued patience and remind them that it can take several weeks before seeing significant improvements at bedtime.

Review of Progress

Discuss the child's progress as a result of the family implementing the selected bedtime intervention. It is important at this time to encourage the accurate reporting of changes they did or did not complete.

In addition, you will need to assess for obstacles to successful bedtime intervention. Several common problems observed when parents try to implement bedtime programs include:

- Lying down with the child until he falls asleep

- Letting the child take naps during the day

- Extended discussions with the child over the rationale for the plan at bedtime

- Interruptions due to illness or other changes (e.g., sleeping away from home)

- Giving in to delay tactics (e.g., asking for another story or something more to drink, etc.)

- Guilt over the child's distress—especially when using graduated extinction

These lapses are not devastating and can be corrected by reinstating the planned steps. The goal is continual progress.

Modifications

Treatment-specific modifications may need to be made to each approach as follows.

Graduated Extinction

If the parents selected a time (for example, 5 minutes) to wait before going into the bedroom and they went in earlier than this on several occasions, you can shorten the time (for example, 3 minutes). Consistency will be more important than the actual time.

If the parents are reluctant to continue this plan because they express concern over causing their child psychological distress or trauma, you can reassure them there is no evidence of any lasting negative consequences when using this technique. If concerns persist, switch to sleep restriction.

If the child becomes so disruptive (e.g., destroying toys, becoming sick) that the parents enter the room early, consider switching to sleep restriction.

Sleep Restriction

If the parents are having a great deal of difficulty keeping the child awake until the new bedtime, consider moving the bedtime somewhat earlier—but still later than the previous bedtime.

If after 3 or more nights the child does not appear tired at the new bedtime—assuming no naps during the day and the wake time is consistent—consider moving the bedtime even later.

If the child engages in increased NREM sleep problems (sleepwalking, sleeptalking, sleep terrors), encourage the parents to be patient, since this is common when a child is initially sleep-deprived. These should abate when the bedtime is moved earlier.

If the child re-experiences bedtime disruption with a change in bedtime (for example, moving from 11:30 P.M. to 11:00 P.M.) move the time back and after a week consider a smaller change in time (for example, 11:15 P.M.).

Remaining Bedtime Issues

If the family wasn't able to implement all the recommendations or there are remaining bedtime issues, outline intervention steps for the coming weeks.

If the problem improved, encourage continued monitoring for at least several weeks to assess effectiveness. If there is no measurable progress after 2 to 3 weeks of implementing intervention steps, consider switching the intervention plan. If the family is unable to make changes, reevaluate the family's ability to implement the current plan.

Homework

✎ If the intervention is producing positive changes at bedtime, have parents continue monitoring using the Sleep Diary and Behavior Log.

✎ Have parents implement new interventions or modify plans as needed.

✎ If other sleep problems are to be addressed, prepare parents to go to the next appropriate module and assign readings and homework.

Module 4
Night Waking

First Session

Reducing Night Waking

(Corresponds to chapter 5 of the workbook)

Materials Needed

- Completed Albany Sleep Problems Scale (ASPS)
- Completed Sleep Intervention Questionnaire (SIQ)
- Completed Sleep Diary
- Completed Behavior Log

Outline

- Set agenda
- Review homework
- Describe intervention options for reducing night waking
- Select the appropriate intervention for the family
- Deal with family resistance, if necessary
- Present steps for graduated extinction (if selected intervention)
- Present steps for sleep restriction (if selected intervention)
- Present steps for scheduled awaking (if selected intervention)
- Assign homework

Setting the Agenda

Provide the family with an overview of the session as well as the expectations for the homework. Encourage their continued patience and remind them that there are a number of different approaches that can be used to successfully improve their child's night waking problems.

Homework Review

Review the completed Sleep Diary and Behavior Log for the past week. Discuss any progress the child has made. If sleep hygiene habits have been changed, determine whether these are having any effect.

Intervention Options

If modifying sleep hygiene habits (especially bedtime routines and sleep-wake schedule) has not been successful in improving night waking problems, the next step is to try one of three interventions: graduated extinction, sleep restriction, and scheduled awakening. The selection among these approaches is based primarily on which one fits best with the family. Begin with a general discussion of the interventions, including their pros and cons.

Graduated Extinction

Graduated extinction involves spending increasingly longer amounts of time ignoring the cries and protests of a child who awakens from sleep. The goal of this treatment is to fade the amount of time the parents attend to the child around night waking while giving them the opportunity to check on their child. The mechanism of change appears to involve forcing the child to learn to fall back to sleep on her own.

Sleep Restriction

Sleep restriction involves reducing the amount of time the child sleeps and then gradually increasing the time to a healthy amount. This can involve moving bedtime later in the evening or waking the child up earlier in the morning. The goal of this treatment is to adjust the sleep amount such that it causes drowsiness and decreases the likelihood of bedtime disturbances. The mechanism of change appears to be creating the conditions (sleep deprivation) that make it easier for the child to practice falling back to sleep without parents present.

Scheduled Awakening

Scheduled awakening involves estimating the time the child typically awakens at night, and waking her up some period of time just prior to the usual time. The goal of this intervention is to have the child fall back asleep from this brief awakening without parental intervention. The mechanism of change for this intervention is unclear, but may involve "reprogramming" the sleep cycle to a more regular sleep-wake schedule and/or giving the child experience in falling asleep alone while drowsy.

Pros and Cons

Use Table 5.1 to help the family consider the advantages and disadvantages of each approach.

Intervention Selection

After describing the interventions, discuss concerns parents may have with each of the approaches. Use their responses to the Sleep Intervention Questionnaire (SIQ) to identify potential obstacles. A review of SIQ categories follows.

Table 5.1 Pros and Cons of Graduated Extinction, Sleep Restriction, and Scheduled Awakening

	Pros	Cons
Graduated Extinction	+ Only needed if and when child awakens + Allows for checking on the child	− Long bouts of crying/tantrums − Can be a temporary increase in crying/tantrums − Not useful for nondisruptive sleep awakening
Sleep Restriction	+ Avoids most crying/tantrums + Can be used for nondisruptive sleep-initiation problems	− Requires family member to stay up later with the child − Can be difficult to keep child awake for new bedtime
Scheduled Awakening	+ Avoids most crying/tantrums + Can be used for nondisruptive sleep-initiation problems	− Requires family member to awaken or stay up later to awaken child − Requires that the night waking(s) occurs at about the same time(s) each evening

Disruption Tolerance

If parents responded "Yes" to one or more of the following questions on the SIQ, they may not be good candidates for graduated extinction.

1. Does your child misbehave at bedtime or when waking up at night in a way that is too serious or upsetting to ignore?

2. Would it be difficult or impossible for you to listen to your child being upset for long periods of time (more than a few minutes)?

3. Do you find it too difficult to put your child back in bed once she gets up?

Schedule Tolerance

If parents responded "No" to one or more of the following questions on the SIQ, then you need to discuss which would be the least disruptive to the family—graduated extinction, sleep restriction, or scheduled awakening.

4. Are you, or another member of your family, willing to stay up later at night to put a sleep plan into action?

5. Are you, or another member of your family, willing to get up earlier in the morning to put a sleep plan into action?

Attitudinal Barriers

A response of "Yes" to one of the following questions on the SIQ may require further intervention with the family to prepare them for any intervention (see the next section on dealing with family resistance).

6. Do you feel emotionally unable to deal directly with your child's sleep problem?

7. Do you feel guilty making your child go to bed (or go back to bed) when she does not want to?

8. Do you think it would be emotionally damaging to your child if you tried to change the way she slept?

Dealing with Family Resistance

Some families require brief cognitive-behavioral intervention to deal with feelings of guilt surrounding their child's sleep problems. You will need to:

1. Assess the ability of parents to intervene at all with their child.

2. Assign, if necessary, just one parent to intervene if the other cannot.

3. Challenge self-talk that interferes with successful intervention (e.g., "My child will be angry with me if I ignore her cries," or "I am a bad parent if my child is upset in the middle of the night.")

4. Determine if more extensive intervention is necessary prior to implementing a sleep plan.

Steps for Graduated Extinction

If graduated extinction is selected as the treatment of choice, follow these steps:

1. Remind the family to maintain a regular bedtime routine.

2. Set an agreed upon bedtime that will not change over the course of the intervention.

3. Negotiate a time for the family to wait before going in to check on their child. A typical time would be between 3–5 minutes the first night.

4. Pick the night to begin the plan, assuming no one will have a good night's sleep that evening—most families begin on a Friday night.

5. On the first night have the parents follow the bedtime routine, put the child to bed at the regular bedtime, leave the room, and then wait the agreed upon time (e.g., 3 minutes) before checking on the child following the night waking.

6. If after waiting the full time the child is still crying upon awakening, parents can go into the room, tell her to go to bed, and then leave. They cannot pick up the child, give her food or a drink, or engage in extensive conversation.

7. Have parents wait the same amount of time (e.g., 3 minutes) before going back into the room each time. They should continue the pattern until the child is asleep or until they feel comfortable waiting longer.

8. On each subsequent night, have parents extend the time between visits by two or three minutes. They should continue the same procedure as in step 6 when returning to the child's room.

Steps for Sleep Restriction

If sleep restriction is selected as the treatment of choice, follow these steps:

1. Select a bedtime when the child is likely to fall asleep with little difficulty and within about 15 minutes. To determine this bedtime, use the Sleep Diary to find a time when the child falls asleep if left alone (e.g., 1 A.M.), then add 30 minutes to this time (e.g, new bedtime = 1:30 A.M.).

2. If the child falls asleep within 15 minutes of being put to bed at this new bedtime and without resistance for 2 successive nights, move back bedtime 15 minutes (e.g., from 1:30 A.M. to 1:15 A.M.).

3. Have parents keep the child awake before the new bedtime, even if she seems to want to fall asleep.

4. If the child does not fall asleep within about 15 minutes after being put to bed, parents should have her leave the bedroom and extend the bedtime for one more hour.

5. Have parents continue to move back the bedtime (e.g., from 1:15 A.M. to 1:00 A.M.) until the desired bedtime is reached.

6. Have parents maintain a regular time to awaken the child and warn them to resist letting the child "sleep in."

Steps for Scheduled Awakening

If scheduled awakening is selected as the treatment of choice, follow these steps:

1. Have the parents use the Sleep Diary to determine the time or times that the child typically awakens during the night.

2. On the night that they are to begin the plan, have them awaken the child approximately 30 minutes prior to the typical awaken-

ing time. For example, if the child usually has a night waking at 12:30 A.M., wake the child at 12:00 A.M. If the child seems to awaken very easily, move the time back by 15 minutes (11:45 P.M.) the next night and on all subsequent nights.

3. If there is a broad range in the times the child awakens (for example, from 12:00 A.M. to 1:30 A.M.), have parents awaken the child about 30 minutes prior to the earliest time (in this case, 11:30 P.M.).

4. Instruct the family not to fully awaken the child. Have them gently touch and/or talk to the child until she opens her eyes, then let her fall back to sleep.

5. Have the family repeat this plan each night until the child goes for a full 7 nights without a waking. If the child has achieved this level of success, have them skip one night (that is, no scheduled waking) during the next week. If the child has awakenings, have them go back to awakening the child every night. They should slowly reduce the number of nights with scheduled awakenings until the child is no longer waking during the night.

Homework

✎ Have parents implement the selected intervention as discussed during the session.

✎ Have parents continue to complete the Sleep Diary on a daily basis.

✎ Have parents continue to complete the Behavior Log as needed.

✎ Assign review of Chapter 5 of the workbook.

Follow-Up Sessions

Night Waking Intervention

(Corresponds to chapter 5 of the workbook)

Materials Needed

- Completed Albany Sleep Problems Scale (ASPS)
- Completed Sleep Intervention Questionnaire (SIQ)
- Completed Sleep Diary
- Completed Behavior Log

Outline

- Set agenda
- Discuss family's progress since last session
- Discuss necessary modifications
- Address remaining night waking issues
- Assign homework

Setting the Agenda

Provide the family with an overview of the session as well as the expectations for the homework. If night waking is still a problem, encourage their continued patience and remind them that it can take several weeks before seeing significant improvements in night waking problems.

Review of Progress

Discuss the child's progress as a result of the family implementing the selected night waking intervention. It is important at this time to encourage the accurate reporting of changes they did or did not complete.

In addition, you will need to assess for obstacles to successful night waking intervention. Several common problems observed when parents try to implement night waking programs include:

- Lying down with the child until she falls back to sleep

- Letting the child take naps during the day

- Extended discussions with the child over the rationale for the plan upon awakening

- Interruptions due to illness or other changes (e.g., sleeping away from home)

- Giving in to avoidance tactics (e.g., asking to sleep in parent's bed)

- Guilt over the child's distress—especially when using graduated extinction

- Skipping scheduled awakenings because of difficulty getting up or reluctance to awaken the child

These lapses are not devastating and can be corrected by re-instating the planned steps. The goal is continual progress.

Modifications

Treatment-specific modifications may need to be made to each approach as follows:

Graduated Extinction

If the parents selected a time (for example, 5 minutes) to wait before going into the bedroom and they went in earlier than this on several occasions, you can shorten the time (for example, 3 minutes). Consistency will be more important than the actual time.

If the parents are reluctant to continue this plan because they express concern over causing their child psychological distress or trauma, you can reassure them there is no evidence of any lasting negative consequences when using this technique. If concerns persist, switch to sleep restriction.

If the child becomes so disruptive (e.g., destroying toys, becoming sick) that the parents enter the room early, consider switching to sleep restriction.

Sleep Restriction

If the parents are having a great deal of difficulty keeping the child awake until the new bedtime, consider moving the bedtime somewhat earlier—but still later than the previous bedtime.

If after 3 or more nights the child does not appear tired at the new bedtime—assuming no naps during the day and the wake time is consistent—consider moving the bedtime even later.

If the child engages in increased NREM sleep problems (sleepwalking, sleeptalking, sleep terrors), encourage the parents to be patient, since this is common when a child is initially sleep deprived. These should abate when the bedtime is moved earlier.

If the child re-experiences bedtime disruption with a change in bedtime (for example, moving from 11:30 P.M. to 11:00 P.M.) move the time back and after a week consider a smaller change in time (for example, 11:15 P.M.).

Scheduled Awakening

If the child fully awakens and does not go back to sleep following awakenings, have the parents move the scheduled awakening time back by 15 minutes for the next episode.

If the parents miss more than an occasional scheduled awakening because they cannot stay up or wake themselves up to do the child awakening, consider switching to another technique.

Remaining Night Waking Issues

If the family wasn't able to implement all the recommendations or there are remaining night waking issues, outline intervention steps for the coming weeks.

If the problem improved, encourage continued monitoring for at least several weeks to assess effectiveness. If there is no measurable progress after 2 to 3 weeks of implementing intervention steps, consider switching the intervention plan. If family is unable to make changes, reevaluate the family's ability to implement the current plan.

Homework

- ✎ If night waking intervention is producing positive changes in sleep, have parents continue monitoring using the Sleep Diary and Behavior Log.

- ✎ Have parents implement new interventions or modify plans as needed.

- ✎ If other sleep problems are to be addressed, prepare parents to go to the next appropriate module and assign readings and homework.

Module 5
Nightmares and Sleep Terrors

First Session

Reducing Nightmares and Sleep Terrors

(Corresponds to chapter 6 of the workbook)

Materials Needed

- Completed Albany Sleep Problems Scale (ASPS)
- Completed Sleep Intervention Questionnaire (SIQ)
- Completed Sleep Diary
- Completed Behavior Log

Outline

- Set agenda
- Review homework
- Differentiate nightmares from sleep terrors
- Describe intervention options for reducing nightmares or sleep terrors
- Select the appropriate intervention
- Deal with family resistance, if necessary
- Present steps for using "magic" (if selected intervention for nightmares)
- Present steps for relaxation (if selected intervention for nightmares)
- Present steps for paradoxical intention (if selected intervention for nightmares)

■ Present steps for scheduled awakening (if selected intervention for sleep terrors)

■ Assign homework

Setting the Agenda

Provide the family with an overview of the session as well as the expectations for the homework. Encourage their continued patience and remind them that there are a number of different approaches that can be used to successfully improve their child's sleep.

Homework Review

Review the completed Sleep Diary and Behavior Log for the past week. Discuss any changes in the child's sleep and sleep problems.

Differentiating Nightmares from Sleep Terrors

Review with parents the nature of nightmares and sleep terrors. Emphasize how these two sleep disturbances are different (see Table 6.1) and that they require different interventions.

Based on the results of the Albany Sleep Problems Scale (ASPS), you should discuss whether the child is experiencing nightmares or sleep terrors and begin to discuss intervention options.

Table 6.1 Differences between Nightmares and Sleep Terrors

NIGHTMARES	SLEEP TERRORS
• Child awakens	• Child asleep
• Child can recall details	• Child has no recall
• Child can be comforted	• Child is difficult to comfort
• Child has limited movement or vocalizations until after waking	• Child may sit up, walk around, or talk during event

Depending on the age of the child, parents can attempt one of three interventions to help reduce anxiety surrounding the—usually transient—problem. For young children (up to about 5 years of age), a cognitive-behavioral intervention in the form of "magic" can be used. For older children, relaxation or paradoxical intervention may be more appropriate.

"Magic"

Using "magic" involves relying on a placebo (for example, a magic wand) to help allay fears the child may have regarding sleep or the content of nightmares. The goal of this treatment is to reduce anxiety about falling asleep and to potentially provide "protection" against feared objects or persons in a nightmare. The mechanism of change appears to involve having the child believe the magical object will be effective, thus relieving anxiety.

Relaxation

Relaxation involves using the technique of progressive muscle relaxation (PMR) before bedtime. The goal of this treatment is to reduce anxiety around sleep or nightmares. The mechanism of change appears to be providing physical and cognitive activities that may be incompatible with anxiety.

Paradoxical Intention

Paradoxical intention involves providing instruction to the child or adolescent to stay awake rather than try to fall asleep. The goal of this intervention is to reduce anxiety surrounding sleep or the anticipation of nightmares. The mechanism of change appears to be providing permission to stay awake that may reduce anxiety around needing to fall asleep.

Intervention Options—Sleep Terrors

Sleep terrors are assumed to be a sign of inadequate sleep and therefore intervention typically takes the form of improving sleep through reducing bedtime problems (see Module 3), reducing night waking (see Module 4), or allowing naps if that does not disrupt the usual sleep pattern. When improving sleep is not successful or cannot be changed quickly, we use scheduled awakening.

Scheduled Awakening

Scheduled awakening involves estimating the time the child typically has a sleep terror, and waking him up some period of time just prior to the usual time. The goal of this intervention is have the child fall back asleep from this brief awakening without parental intervention. The mechanism of change for this intervention is unclear but may involve "reprogramming" the sleep cycle to a more regular sleep-wake schedule.

Intervention Selection

Again for nightmares, using "magic" is appropriate for younger children. If the child or adolescent is anxious at bedtime, relaxation can be attempted. If the anxiety is primarily cognitive (e.g., obsessing about school), paradoxical instruction may be appropriate.

For night terrors, improving sleep is usually the first step. If methods to improve sleep are not adequate, then scheduled awakening is employed.

Dealing with Family Resistance

Some families require brief cognitive-behavioral intervention to deal with feelings of guilt surrounding their child's sleep problems. You will need to:

1. Assess the ability of parents to intervene at all with their child.

2. Assign, if necessary, just one parent to intervene if the other cannot.

3. Challenge self-talk that interferes with successful intervention (e.g., "I must be doing something wrong if my child has nightmares/sleep terrors.")

4. Determine if more extensive intervention is necessary prior to implementing a sleep plan.

Steps for "Magic"

If "magic" is selected as the treatment of choice for nightmares, follow these steps:

1. Remind the family to maintain a regular bedtime routine.

2. Set an agreed upon bedtime that will not change over the course of the intervention.

3. Find an age-appropriate item (for example, "magic wand," toy sword, "magic dust") that might help the child feel more in control (for example, by using a sword to fight off monsters).

4. Have the parents introduce the magic item each evening, emphasizing how powerful it is and that it will, eventually, help the child deal with scary dreams.

5. Have the parents encourage the child to discuss the magic item and how it could help him.

Steps for Relaxation

If relaxation is selected as the treatment of choice for nightmares, follow these steps:

1. Remind the family to maintain a regular bedtime routine.

2. Set an agreed upon bedtime that will not change over the course of the intervention.

3. Instruct the parents to make relaxation training the last part of the bedtime routine.

4. Have the family begin by telling the child to lie back on his bed. Arms and legs should be limp as well as the head. Remind them that if the child is holding up his head, this means that the muscles of the neck are tensing and he cannot be completely relaxed.

5. For younger children, or children who seem to have a problem following the directions, a simple instruction such as "act like a wet noodle" may be enough to help them visualize what is needed.

6. Instruct the parents to begin with the facial muscles, asking the child to slowly and carefully tense the muscles. The tension of the muscles should last for about 5 seconds.

7. Following the tension of a set of muscles, parents should have the child relax the muscles, and give him 10–15 seconds to experience the good feeling of relaxation.

8. Remind parents to talk to their child using a soothing and calming voice, and take their time.

9. The exercise moves from the facial muscles to the jaw (clenching and relaxing the jaw), then to the neck and shoulders, arms and hands, chest, stomach, thighs, legs, and feet.

10. Tell parents to have the child tell them if he experiences any pain or discomfort. They may need to instruct him not to tense the muscles too tightly, or they may want to avoid certain muscle groups.

11. Instruct parents to have the child practice until he can run through it alone.

12. Instruct parents to use the technique at bedtime and any time the child feels tense or anxious.

Steps for Paradoxical Intention

If paradoxical intention is selected as the treatment of choice for nightmares, follow these steps:

1. Remind the family to maintain a regular bedtime routine.

2. Set an agreed upon bedtime that will not change over the course of the intervention.

3. Instruct the parents to make paradoxical intention the last part of the bedtime routine.

4. Have parents begin by telling the child or adolescent to lie back on his bed.

5. Parents should inform the child or adolescent that they want him to try to stay awake; however, if he falls asleep, that's okay—they don't want the child or adolescent to be anxious that he will fall asleep.

6. The child or adolescent should remain in bed in the dark, lying still and relaxed with his eyes closed.

7. The parents should try to assess how much sleep the child or adolescent received each night.

Steps for Scheduled Awakening

If scheduled awakening is selected as the treatment of choice for sleep terrors, follow these steps:

1. Have the parents use the Sleep Diary to determine the time or times that the child typically has a sleep terror during the night.

2. On the night that parents are to begin the plan, have them awaken the child approximately 30 minutes prior to the typical time for a sleep terror. For example, if the child usually has a sleep terror at 12:30 A.M., wake the child at 12:00 A.M. If the child seems to awaken very easily, move the time back by 15 minutes (11:45 P.M.) the next night and on all subsequent nights.

3. If there is a broad range in the times the child has sleep terrors (for example, from 12:00 A.M. to 1:30 A.M.), awaken the child about 30 minutes prior to the earliest time (in this case, 11:30 P.M.).

4. Instruct the family not to fully awaken the child. Have them gently touch and/or talk to the child until he opens his eyes, then let him fall back to sleep.

5. Have the family repeat this plan each night until the child goes for a full 7 nights without a sleep terror. If the child has achieved this level of success, have them skip one night (that is, no scheduled waking) during the next week. If the child has sleep terrors, have them go back to awakening the child every night. They should slowly reduce the number of nights with scheduled awakenings until the child is no longer experiencing sleep terrors.

Homework

✎ Have parents implement the selected intervention as discussed during the session.

✎ Have parents continue to complete the Sleep Diary on a daily basis.

✎ Have parents continue to complete the Behavior Log as needed.

✎ Assign review of Chapter 6 of the workbook.

Follow-Up Sessions

Interventions for Nightmares and Sleep Terrors

(Corresponds to chapter 6 of the workbook)

Materials Needed

- Completed Albany Sleep Problems Scale (ASPS)
- Completed Sleep Intervention Questionnaire (SIQ)
- Completed Sleep Diary
- Completed Behavior Log

Outline

- Set agenda
- Discuss family's progress since last session
- Discuss necessary modifications
- Address remaining issues with nightmares or sleep terrors
- Assign homework

Setting the Agenda

Provide the family with an overview of the session as well as the expectations for the homework. If nightmares or sleep terrors are still a problem, encourage their continued patience and remind them that it can take several weeks before seeing significant improvements in sleep.

Discuss the child's progress as a result of the family implementing the selected intervention. It is important at this time to encourage the accurate reporting of changes they did or did not complete.

In addition, you will need to assess for obstacles to successful nightmare intervention. Several common problems observed when parents try to implement a program for nightmares include:

- Lying down with the child until he falls asleep or falls back to sleep

- Interruptions due to illness or other changes (sleeping away from home)

- Guilt over their child's distress

- Expecting change too quickly

These lapses are not devastating and can be corrected by reinstating the planned steps. The goal is continual progress.

Modifications

If the parents are reluctant to continue the intervention plan because they express concern that their child will have psychological distress or trauma resulting from the nightmares, you can reassure them there is no evidence of any lasting negative consequences for occasional nightmares. Treatment specific modifications may need to be made as follows.

"Magic"

If the parents and child selected an object or routine that does not seem to work, encourage them to brainstorm alternative strategies. Sometimes the second try works best.

Relaxation

If the child or adolescent is having trouble relaxing—especially if he cannot turn off his thoughts—encourage the use of soothing music to accompany the muscle relaxation.

Paradoxical Intention

If the child or adolescent is anxious about trying to stay awake, consider switching to relaxation.

Review of Progress—Sleep Terrors

Discuss child's progress as a result of the family implementing the selected sleep terrors intervention. It is important at this time to encourage the accurate reporting of changes they did or did not complete.

In addition, you will need to assess for obstacles to successful sleep terrors intervention. Several common problems observed when parents try to implement sleep terrors programs include:

- Skipping scheduled awakenings because of difficulty getting up or reluctance to awaken the child

- Interruptions due to illness or other changes (e.g., sleeping away from home)

- Guilt over the child's distress

These lapses are not devastating and can be corrected by reinstating the planned steps. The goal is continual progress.

Modifications

Treatment-specific modifications for scheduled awakening may need to be made as follows.

If the child fully awakens and does not go back to sleep following awakenings, have the parents move the scheduled awakening time back by 15 minutes for the next episode.

If the parents miss more than an occasional scheduled awakening because they cannot stay up or wake themselves up to do the child awakening, consider switching to another technique (for example, other techniques used to improve overall sleep such as sleep restriction—see Module 2).

Remaining Issues

If the family wasn't able to implement all the recommendations or there are remaining issues with nightmares or sleep terrors, outline intervention steps for the coming weeks.

If the problem improved, encourage continued monitoring for at least several weeks to assess effectiveness. If there is no measurable progress after 2 to 3 weeks of implementing intervention steps, consider switching the intervention plan. If the family is unable to make changes, reevaluate the family's ability to implement the current plan.

Homework

✎ If the intervention is producing positive changes in sleep, have parents continue monitoring using the Sleep Diary and Behavior Log.

✎ Have parents implement new interventions or modify plans as needed.

✎ If other sleep-related issues are to be addressed, prepare parents to go to the next appropriate module and assign readings and homework.

Module 6
Bedwetting

First Session

Addressing Bedwetting

(Corresponds to chapter 7 of the workbook)

Materials Needed

- Bedwetting Recording Sheet

- Completed Albany Sleep Problems Scale (ASPS)

- Completed Sleep Intervention Questionnaire (SIQ)

Outline

- Set agenda

- Introduce causes of bedwetting

- Instruct parents on initial steps

- Introduce Bedwetting Recording Sheet

- Assign homework

Setting the Agenda

Provide the family with an overview of the session as well as the expectations for the homework. Encourage their continued patience and remind them that there are a number of different approaches that can be used to successfully reduce their child's bedwetting.

Though bedwetting is not classified as a sleep problem, we address it in this book because it is a common nighttime occurrence—seen in up to 20% of school-aged children (Safarinejad, in press). Successful toilet training typically occurs between the ages of 2½ and 4. It is normal for young children to have occasional incidents of bedwetting; however, by age 6, children should be able to sleep through the night without accidents.

Bedwetting or nocturnal enuresis is categorized as either 1) primary (child who has never successfully had bladder control at night) or 2) secondary (the loss of bladder control at night after a period of time—at least 3–6 months of no accidents). The secondary form of enuresis sometimes occurs as a result of some medical problem (for example, a bladder infection) or because of some emotional upset, such as a pending divorce by the parents.

Causes of bedwetting may be physical or psychological and can involve:

■ Urinary tract infections and other medical conditions

■ Chronic constipation

■ Lack of antidiuretic hormone or ADH

■ Stress and emotional upset

Because of the possible role of medical causes of bedwetting, every child should be screened by a physician prior to developing a plan.

Initial Steps

For some 80% of children, physical problems are not the cause of their bedwetting (Safarinejad, in press). As a result, a variety of techniques have been used to help children learn (and sometimes re-learn) how to avoid wetting the bed at night. Before any specific techniques are recommended, however, it is usually suggested that parents take the following steps:

■ Limit the child's fluids prior to bedtime and cut down on drinks or foods with caffeine, which can cause more urination.

- Have the child stop in the bathroom right before going to sleep.

- Punishment, in the form of yelling, nagging, or ridicule, should not be used for accidents, and can make the problem worse.

- If an accident occurs, have the child participate in the clean-up, but again, this should not be done in a punishing way.

If these small steps are not enough, then several more formal techniques can be presented as possible aids for bedwetting during the second session.

Introduction of Bedwetting Recording Sheet

A Bedwetting Recording Sheet is used to assist parents keep track of the frequency of bedwetting for their child. In addition, space is available for parents to record how they respond to accidents. This can help you determine how they typically react to bedwetting and what about their response will need to change. See Figure 7.1 for an example.

Two weeks of data recording is an ideal length for observing trends. If bedwetting occurs at a stable rate—such as every night—then one week's worth of data should be sufficient for a pretreatment baseline. The corresponding workbook chapter includes a blank copy of the Bedwetting Recording Sheet. Additional blank forms are provided in an appendix to the workbook—you may photocopy extra forms as needed.

Homework

- ✎ Have parents get their child screened by a physician for possible medical causes of bedwetting.

- ✎ Have parents implement initial steps for handling bedwetting.

- ✎ Have parents complete the Bedwetting Recording Sheet each night.

- ✎ Assign review of Chapter 7 of the workbook.

Bedwetting Recording Sheet

Child's Name: Michael

Dates of Recording: September 3–9

Day of the Week	Time of Bedwetting	Response
Monday	1:30 a.m.	Helped him wash up and change his clothes and sheets – he then slept in our bed
Tuesday	12:15 a.m.	Changed his clothes and sheets and comforted him
Wednesday		No bedwetting
Thursday		
Friday		
Saturday		
Sunday		

Figure 7.1.

Example of Completed Bedwetting Recording Sheet

Second Session

Reducing Bedwetting

(Corresponds to chapter 7 of the workbook)

Materials Needed

- Completed Bedwetting Recording Sheet

- Completed Albany Sleep Problems Scale (ASPS)

- Completed Sleep Intervention Questionnaire (SIQ)

Outline

- Set agenda

- Review homework

- Describe intervention options for bedwetting

- Select the appropriate intervention for the family

- Deal with family resistance, if necessary

- Present steps for the "bell and pad" technique

- Present steps for dry bed training

- Present steps for full-spectrum home training

- Discuss medical treatments for bedwetting

- Assign homework

Setting the Agenda

If a doctor has screened the child and found no physical problems present, continue with the bedwetting module. Provide the family with an overview of the session as well as the expectations for the homework. Encourage their continued patience and remind them that there are a number of different approaches that can be used to successfully reduce their child's bedwetting.

Homework Review

Review the Bedwetting Recording Sheet for the past week. Discuss any changes that have occurred as a result of the family carrying out the initial steps for dealing with bedwetting.

Intervention Options

There are several different techniques that can be tried for bedwetting problems: the "bell and pad" technique, dry bed training, and full-spectrum home training. Give the parents an overview of each of the techniques as follows.

The "Bell and Pad" Technique

A urine alarm, or the "bell and pad", is one of the oldest techniques for helping children with enuresis. This commercially available device consists of a pad that goes underneath the child's sheet. If the pad gets wet, it sets off an alarm that is loud enough to wake the child (and the family), and the child is directed to finish urinating in the bathroom. Then parents help the child clean her clothes and bed (cleanliness tranining).

This simple technique alone has proven helpful to up to 75% of children who participate in this type of plan (Oredsson & Jorgensen, 1998). On the down side, a significant number of children who do at first succeed with the use of the bell and pad may relapse, or begin again to have bedwetting problems.

Dry Bed Training

Dry bed training includes the use of the bell and pad, and cleanliness training, along with steps for scheduled awakenings. On the first night of dry bed training, the child is awakened each hour, brought to the bathroom, and encouraged to urinate. Then the child is given something to drink and is asked to try to hold it in until she is awakened again. Finally, the child is allowed to return to bed. On the second night of this plan, the child is awakened only once, 3 hours after going to bed, and is again encouraged to urinate, given something to drink, and returned to bed. For each subsequent night that the child succeeds in staying dry, the waking time is moved back one half hour until it reaches one hour after bedtime. In addition, a positive practice procedure is used in which parents ask their child to lie in bed, count up to 50, and then get up, go into the bathroom, and try to urinate.

Full-Spectrum Home Training

Full-spectrum home training (FSHT) includes the bell and pad, and cleanliness training. It also uses two additional techniques to try to help the child stay dry once the program is completed. A "retention control training" procedure is taught to the child during the day in a manner similar to the positive practice part of dry bed training. The final part of the FSHT package is an "overlearning" component. This part of the plan is specifically designed to help children with the problem of relapse and begins after the child has been dry for 14 consecutive nights. Following this 2-week success, the child is given fluids before bedtime to help strengthen the ability to stay dry overnight.

Intervention Selection

After describing the interventions, discuss concerns that parents may have with each of the approaches. Typically, the simplest approach (the bell and pad) is introduced first, followed by the other procedures.

Dealing with Family Resistance

Some families require brief cognitive-behavioral intervention to deal with feelings of guilt surrounding their child's bedwetting problems. You will need to:

1. Assess the ability of parents to intervene at all with their child.

2. Assign, if necessary, just one parent to intervene if the other cannot.

3. Challenge self-talk that interferes with successful intervention (e.g., "My child will be angry with me if I make her change clothes," or "I am a bad parent if my child wets the bed."),

4. Determine if more extensive intervention is necessary prior to implementing a bedwetting plan.

Steps for the "Bell and Pad" Technique

Families can purchase the equipment for the bell and pad technique from a number of different online sources (for example, http://www.bed wettingstore.com); it is also sometimes available at department stores such as Sears. Review the following steps with the parents, making sure they are clear about how to implement each portion of the program:

1. Instruct parents to hook up the alarm themselves each night. Some children are embarrassed and may not be reliable to set it up themselves. Have them test it by touching the sensors (it's safe) with a wet finger.

2. Have parents listen for the alarm carefully and respond to it quickly.

3. Tell parents to have a night-light or flashlight nearby so they will be able to see what they are doing when the alarm sounds.

4. As soon as parents hear the alarm, they are to get out of bed and turn off the alarm.

5. Parents should then have the child go to the bathroom and finish urinating.

6. Once finished, parents should help the child clean her clothes and bed.

7. Parents should use the alarm every night until the child experiences 3 or 4 consecutive weeks without bedwetting. This can take 2 to 3 months, so warn them to be patient.

Steps for Dry Bed Training

If the bell and pad technique was not successful by itself, or the child relapses, consider recommending dry bed training—which includes the use of the bell and pad along with several other steps. Review the following steps with the parents, making sure they are clear about how to implement each portion of the program:

1. Have the family establish a nightly waking schedule. On the first night, the child is awakened each and every hour. On the second night, the child is awakened three hours after going to bed. If the child is dry for the remainder of that night, then the waking is moved back to 2½ hours after bedtime. The waking time continues moving back for each dry night until it is 1 hour after bedtime. If the child wets the bed 2 or more times in 1 week, the schedule is restarted.

2. Upon awaking the child, parents should bring the child to the bathroom and ask her to urinate.

3. After the bathroom trip, the parents should give the child some fluids to drink and ask her to try to hold it in until the next awakening.

4. Parents allow the child to return to bed until the next awakening.

Positive Practice Procedure

At the same time, have the family begin a positive practice procedure. Instruct parents to ask their child to lie in bed, count up to 50, and then get up, go into the bathroom, and try to urinate. This should be repeated

20 times—both right after each instance of wetting the bed and again the next night at bedtime.

Bell and Pad Procedure and Cleanliness Training

Also, have the family install the bell and pad on the second night of the waking schedule. If the child wets the bed after the first night of using the bell and pad and the alarm goes off, have parents instruct the child to change the wet clothes and remove the wet sheets from the bed. The child should then be directed to get dressed and make the bed. This last step is repeated 20 times for each instance of bedwetting before the child can go back to sleep. Repeatedly taking off and putting on clothes and remaking the bed is unpleasant and is thought to help the child avoid accidents.

Steps for Full-Spectrum Home Training

If either of the previous procedures was not successful or the child relapses, consider recommending full-spectrum home training. This technique includes the bell and pad procedure as well as two additional techniques to try to help the child stay dry once the program is completed. Review the following steps with the parents, making sure they are clear about how to implement each portion of the program.

Bell and Pad Procedure and Cleanliness Training

Have the parents install the bell and pad and begin procedure. If the child wets the bed after the first night and the alarm goes off, instruct the parents to have their child change out of her wet clothes and remove the wet sheets from the bed. The child should then be directed to get dressed and make the bed. This last step is repeated 20 times for each instance of bedwetting before the child can go back to sleep.

Retention Control Training

At the same time as starting the bell and pad procedure, instruct the parents to give their child a large amount of fluids at bedtime. Then when the child indicates that she has to urinate, they should ask her to hold it for three minutes. Afterwards, the parents should give their child some tangible reward (such as money or some other prize) for successfully holding urination. They should increase the time by three minutes each day until the child can hold her urination for 45 minutes, at which point training ends. If the child fails on one day, they should repeat the same amount of time the next day.

Overlearning Component

After 14 consecutive successful (dry) nights, instruct the parents to start the overlearning component of training. The steps are as follows:

1. Have parents give their child 2 ounces of water in the 15 minutes before bedtime on the first night, and add 2 ounces for each 2 consecutive dry nights.

2. If the child has an accident, the amount of water should be cut back by 2 ounces.

3. Parents should stop adding more water when the maximum for the child is reached. The maximum number of ounces is determined by adding 2 to the child's age in years (e.g., if the child is 6 years old, the maximum number of ounces is 8).

4. Overlearning ends when the child has had 14 consecutive dry nights while drinking the maximum fluids prior to bedtime.

One advantage of the full-spectrum home training program may be in its ability to reduce relapse among children. Research suggests that less than half of the children using this plan relapse as compared to those on the other plans presented (Barclay & Houts, 1995). This plan, like dry bed training, requires a significant commitment by the family, and it can be several months before complete success is achieved.

Medical treatments have been used over the years to help children who have difficulty with nighttime wetting. One medical approach to the treatment of bedwetting involves the use of the drug desmopressin acetate. This drug is an artificially produced form of the body's natural antidiuretic hormone (ADH) that seems to be underproduced by some children who experience bedwetting problems. Desmopressin acetate is given to children in a nasal spray, and older children can learn to give themselves the medication when it is needed. This drug provides a substitute for natural ADH and helps the child's body make less urine, reducing the risk of nighttime accidents. Research to date suggests improvements in bedwetting comparable to using the bell and pad technique, although the results may not last once the medication is removed (Makari & Rushton, 2006).

Tricyclic drugs such as imipramine and desipramine can be effective in initially reducing bedwetting, although their positive effects seem to disappear when the child stops taking the medication (Makari & Rushton, 2006). It is thought that the drug may relax muscles around the bladder, which should help it hold more fluid for a longer period of time. Also, another effect of this drug is that it suppresses REM or dream sleep. This interruption of normal sleep may also help children with bladder control. A number of adverse side effects are associated with these medications (including anorexia, anxiety, constipation, depression, diarrhea, irritability, sleep disturbance, and upset stomach) and therefore the decision to use these medications should be made cautiously. Families interested in trying medication should speak with their doctor.

Homework

✎ Have parents implement the selected intervention as discussed during the session.

✎ Have parents continue to complete the Bedwetting Recording Sheet each night.

Follow-Up Sessions

Bedwetting Intervention

(Corresponds to chapter 7 of the workbook)

Materials Needed

- Completed Bedwetting Recording Sheet
- Completed Albany Sleep Problems Scale (ASPS)
- Completed Sleep Intervention Questionnaire (SIQ)

Outline

- Set agenda
- Discuss family's progress since last session
- Address remaining bedwetting issues
- Assign homework

Setting the Agenda

Provide the family with an overview of the session as well as the expectations for the homework. If bedwetting is still a problem, encourage their continued patience and remind them that it can take several months before seeing significant improvements.

Review of Progress

Discuss the child's progress as a result of the family implementing the selected intervention. It is important at this time to encourage the accurate reporting of changes they did or did not complete.

In addition, you will need to assess for obstacles to successful bedwetting intervention. Several common problems observed when parents try to implement a program for bedwetting include:

- Interruptions due to illness or other changes (e,g., sleeping away from home)

- Guilt over the child's distress

- Expecting change too quickly

These lapses are not devastating and can be corrected by reinstating the planned steps. The goal is continual progress.

Remaining Bedwetting Issues

If the family wasn't able to implement all the recommendations or there are remaining bedwetting issues, outline intervention steps for the coming weeks.

If the problem improved, encourage continued monitoring for at least several weeks to assess effectiveness. If there is no measurable progress after 2 to 3 months of implementing intervention steps, consider switching the intervention plan. If the family is unable to make changes, reevaluate the family's ability to implement the current plan.

Homework

✎ If the bedwetting intervention is producing positive changes, have parents continue monitoring using the Bedwetting Recording Sheet.

✎ Have parents implement new interventions as needed.

✎ If other sleep-related issues are to be addressed, prepare parents to go to the next appropriate module and assign readings and homework.

Module 7
Other Sleep-Related Issues

Improving Other Sleep-Related Problems

(Corresponds to chapter 8 of the workbook)

Materials Needed

- Completed Albany Sleep Problems Scale (ASPS)

- Completed Sleep Intervention Questionnaire (SIQ)

- Completed Sleep Diary

- Completed Behavior Log

Outline

- Set agenda

- Review homework

- Differentiate and discuss other sleep-related problems

- Describe intervention options for reducing sleepwalking and related problems

- Describe intervention options for improving problems related to sleeping at the wrong times

- Identify possible causes of excessive sleepiness

- Identify other nighttime problems or concerns

- Select the appropriate intervention for the family

- Assign homework

Setting the Agenda

Provide the family with an overview of the session as well as the expectations for the homework. Encourage their continued patience and remind them that there are a number of different approaches that can be used to successfully improve their child's sleep.

Homework Review

Review the completed Sleep Diary and Behavior Log for the past week. Discuss any changes in the child's sleep and sleep-related problems.

Differentiating Other Sleep-Related Problems

Based on the results of the Albany Sleep Problems Scale (ASPS), you should discuss whether the child is experiencing sleepwalking (or related events such as sleeptalking or sleepeating), sleeping at the wrong times, or excessive sleepiness. Additionally, other nighttime problems (e.g., teeth grinding) or concerns that can interfere with sleep (e.g., anxiety, depression, or headaches) should be addressed.

Intervention Options—Sleepwalking and Related Problems

Sleepwalking, sleeptalking, and other related problems (including sleepeating) are sleep disturbances that most often occur during non-dream or NREM sleep, usually within the first few hours after falling asleep at night. In children, the causes of these active sleep events have been thought to include anxiety, a lack of sleep, and fatigue. They have also been linked to seizure disorders, which should be ruled out by a physician. For the most part, these sleep events should not be a source of concern. However, there are occasional reports of people harming themselves or others during sleepwalking, and therefore some precautions should be taken if this is a frequent occurrence. Strategies to reduce these problem sleep events include:

■ Encourage more sleep and generally try to make sure that the child is fully rested

- Identify and address potential sources of stress or anxiety

- If more sleep is not possible or effective a trial of scheduled awakening may prove helpful

Steps for Scheduled Awakening

If scheduled awakening is selected as the treatment of choice, follow these steps:

1. Have the parents use the Sleep Diary to determine the time(s) that the child typically awakens during the night with these sleep events.

2. On the night that parents are to begin the plan, have them awaken the child approximately 30 minutes prior to the typical time for the sleep episode. For example, if the child usually walks in her sleep at 12:30 A.M., wake up the child at 12:00 A.M. If the child seems to awaken very easily, move back the time 15 minutes the next night and on all subsequent nights (11:45 P.M.).

3. If there is a broad range in the times for the sleep episode (for example, from 12:00 A.M. to 1:30 A.M.), have the parents awaken the child about 30 minutes prior to the earliest time (in this case, 11:30 P.M.).

4. Instruct the family not to fully awaken the child. Have them gently touch and/or talk to the child until he opens his eyes, then let him fall back to sleep.

5. Have the family repeat this plan each night until the child goes for a full 7 nights without the sleep disturbance. If the child has achieved this level of success, have them skip one night (that is, no scheduled waking) during the next week. If the child has another episode, have them go back to awakening the child every night. They should slowly reduce the number of nights with scheduled awakenings until the child is no longer experiencing problems.

Some children have difficulty falling asleep at the desired time in the evening and waking up at the right time the next morning, not because of resistance to sleep but, rather, as a result of desynchronization between the child's biological clock and the external world. Generally referred to as *circadian rhythm disorders,* these difficulties can be particularly disruptive and include:

Delayed Sleep Phase Syndrome—inability to fall asleep at night, staying up later and waking up later than usual

Advanced Sleep Phase Syndrome—falling asleep too early and waking up earlier than desired in the morning

Non-24-Hour Sleep-Wake Cycles—having a sleep-wake cycle not following the typical 24-hour period, causing a gradual shift in sleep-wake times (for example, falling asleep later and later each night until the child is sleeping during the day and awake at night)

General Strategies

The following strategies can be tried if "sleep hygiene" (described in Module 2) is not successful in realigning the child's sleep times. However, more serious or treatment-resistant sleep-cycle problems should be referred to a sleep expert.

Arrange daily activity cues. All typical daily activities (e.g., meals, bathing, homework, etc.) should occur during normal times. Instruct parents not to adapt these schedules to meet the needs of the child's disrupted sleep—such as allowing the child to eat dinner at 2 A.M.—so that the daily activity cues help the child readjust his sleep schedule.

Experiment with melatonin. Instruct the family (in consultation with child's pediatrician) to try giving the child melatonin about 30 minutes prior to the desired bedtime. This can sometimes help reset the biological clock such that the child sleeps on a more regular schedule.

Bright light therapy. A typical bright light therapy plan involves having the child sit in front of a bank of lights for several hours after awaking. The lights must provide more light than is typical in a home or at school because they have to produce approximately the amount of light provided by the sun. "Light boxes" are now commercially available and usually include about six florescent light tubes. The child sits facing these lights and can work or carry on other activities at the same time. Using these lights has helped some people regulate their sleep cycles toward one that better matches a typical sleep schedule.

If these steps are unsuccessful, two other approaches—sleep restriction and chronotherapy—can be useful. Chronotherapy requires a major time commitment on the part of the family and is usually the approach of last resort. These two approaches are described next.

Sleep Restriction

Sleep restriction involves reducing the amount of time the child sleeps and then gradually increasing the time back to a healthy amount. This can involve moving bedtime later in the evening or waking the child up earlier in the morning. This technique works by resetting the child's biological clock. Follow these steps:

1. Select a bedtime when the child is likely to fall asleep with little difficulty and within about 15 minutes. To determine this bedtime, use the Sleep Diary to find a time when the child falls asleep if left alone (e.g., 1 A.M.), then add 30 minutes to this time (new bedtime = 1:30 A.M.).

2. If the child falls asleep within 15 minutes of being put to bed at this new bedtime and without resistance for 2 successive nights, move the bedtime back by 15 minutes (from 1:30 A.M. to 1:15 A.M.).

3. Have parents keep the child awake before the new bedtime, even if he seems to want to fall asleep.

4. If the child does not fall asleep within about 15 minutes after being put to bed, have him leave the bedroom and extend the bedtime for one more hour.

5. Continue to move back the bedtime (e.g., from 1:15 A.M. to 1:00 A.M.) until the desired bedtime is reached.

6. Have parents maintain a regular time to awaken the child and warn them to resist letting the child "sleep in."

Chronotherapy

Chronotherapy essentially involves keeping the child awake later and later on successive nights, until he achieves the desired new sleep schedule. If chronotherapy is selected as the treatment of choice, follow these steps:

- Have the parents use the Sleep Diary to identify the typical sleep-wake schedule for their child.

- On the night parents are to begin the plan, have them keep the child awake approximately 3 hours after his typical bedtime. For example, if the child usually falls asleep at 1:00 A.M., they should keep the child up until 4:00 A.M.

- Instruct the parents not to allow the child to sleep at times other than the scheduled ones—that is, no naps.

- Each successive night parents should move the bedtime ahead by another 3 hours (for example, from 3:00 A.M. to 6:00 A.M.).

- Parents should keep this schedule until their child's new bedtime approximates the desired bedtime (for example, 10:00 P.M.).

Unfortunately, what this plan offers in terms of its simplicity is usually offset by its lack of practicality. For most families it would be extremely difficult if not impossible to adhere to this type of sleep schedule. The demands of school, work, and family would prohibit following a schedule that would, for a time, have the child remain awake at night and sleep during the day. For this reason chronotherapy is not often recommended unless all other reasonable options have been tried and have failed. Even then, implementing such a plan might have to wait until an unstructured time, such as a summer vacation, makes it possible to begin such a strategy.

Excessive Sleepiness

A child who displays excessive sleepiness such that it interferes with daily activities and that cannot be attributed to other sleep problems (such as night waking or insufficient sleep) should be assessed by a sleep or other medical professional. The responses of the parents on the Albany Sleep Problems Scale (ASPS) can be used to help identify the nature of a child's excessive sleepiness. Scores on specific questions can point to one of the following concerns: hypersomnia, narcolepsy, breathing-related sleep disorders, or limb movement disorders.

Hypersomnia and Narcolepsy

Hypersomnia is a problem of sleeping too much. Despite getting a full night's sleep each evening, some children (and adults) find themselves falling asleep several times each day. Narcolepsy is a serious sleep problem that includes uncontrollable sleep attacks as well as daytime sleepiness. People with narcolepsy experience cataplexy, or a sudden loss of muscle tone. These are not seizures, but instead are involuntary sleep attacks.

Breathing-Related Sleep Disorders

Difficulties in breathing can result in numerous brief arousals throughout the night so that the child does not feel rested even after 8 or 9 hours "asleep." At the extreme end, sleep apnea involves periods where the child stops breathing completely—again, interrupting sleep. Often there is no recollection of these breathing problems upon waking.

Limb Movement Disorders

Physical movements, such as leg and arm twitching, that continue throughout most of the night may interrupt sleep, even without the child being aware of their occurrence. Two types of movement-related sleep problems are relatively common causes of daytime sleepiness: periodic limb movements and restless legs syndrome. Medical evaluation and intervention is recommended for these problems.

Other Nighttime Problems

Responses on the Albany Sleep Problems Scale (ASPS) can be used to identify other nighttime problems that may require intervention. Some of these concerns are outlined here.

Problems with Anxiety

Being anxious can have a direct impact on how one sleeps and can include 1) anxiety about daytime issues (for example, school) or 2) anxiety about not being able to sleep. Anxiety about sleeping itself can be helped by using a form of paradoxical instruction. Instruct the family to go through the usual bedtime routine, but tell the child that falling asleep is not that important. The child should be in bed, with the lights out, and with eyes closed. However, the child should be told to try to remain awake without opening his eyes or moving around too much. If the child is anxious about not being able to sleep, giving him permission to stay awake can help relieve these fears and paradoxically help the child fall asleep.

Problems with Depression

Being depressed can seriously interfere with sleep—either causing too much sleep or not enough. If depression is suspected as interfering with sleep, referral for treatment should be made.

Sleep-Related Headaches

Some children experience headaches when they wake up in the morning. There are at least three common causes for early-morning headaches: breathing difficulties, caffeine withdrawal, or sleep deprivation. Specific interventions for each of these causes should be explored.

Rhythmic Movement Disorder

Some children rock back and forth in their beds before going to sleep. Sometimes this rocking includes head banging against the wall or the side of the crib. In all of these cases, parents usually report that the rocking or head banging seems to be soothing to their child and that it helps them fall asleep. These types of behaviors are more formally referred to as rhythmic movement disorder, and they are fairly common (in their less injurious forms) among infants and toddlers. Often no intervention is necessary. If treatment is desired, sleep restriction can be helpful (see steps for sleep restriction under "Intervention Options—Sleeping at the Wrong Times").

Nighttime Teeth Grinding (Nocturnal Bruxism)

This includes all forms of teeth clenching and grinding that occur during sleep. This does not seem to be a serious sleep concern on its own; however, the dental consequences (grinding down of the teeth) can become serious in children who frequently grind their teeth. In addition, people who grind their teeth are more likely to have jaw pain and headaches than those who have no teeth grinding. Referral to a pediatrician is recommended for evaluation and intervention.

Homework

✎ Have parents implement the selected intervention as discussed during the session.

✎ Have parents seek an evaluation by a sleep expert or pediatrician if necessary.

✎ Have parents continue to complete the Sleep Diary on a daily basis.

✎ Have parents continue to complete the Behavior Log as needed.

✎ Assign review of relevant sections of Chapter 8 of the workbook.

Follow-Up Sessions

Interventions for Sleep-Related Problems

(Corresponds to chapter 8 of the workbook)

Materials Needed

- Completed Albany Sleep Problems Scale (ASPS)

- Completed Sleep Intervention Questionnaire (SIQ)

- Completed Sleep Diary

- Completed Behavior Log

Outline

- Set agenda

- Discuss family's progress since last session

- Address remaining sleep-related issues

- Assign homework

Setting the Agenda

Provide the family with an overview of the session as well as the expectations for the homework. If there are still other sleep-related problems, encourage their continued patience and remind them that it can take several weeks before seeing significant improvements.

Review of Progress

Discuss the child's progress as a result of the family implementing the selected intervention. It is important at this time to encourage the accurate reporting of changes they did or did not complete.

Remaining Sleep-Related Issues

If the family wasn't able to implement all the recommendations or there are other sleep-related issues, outline interventions steps for the coming weeks.

If the sleep-related problem improved, encourage continued monitoring for at least several weeks to assess effectiveness. If there is no measurable progress after 2 to 3 weeks of implementing intervention steps, consider switching the intervention plan. If family is unable to make changes, reevaluate the family's ability to implement the current plan.

Homework

✎ If the intervention is producing positive changes, have parents continue monitoring using the Sleep Diary and Behavior Log.

✎ Have parents implement new or additional interventions as needed.

✎ Assign any remaining readings or homework as appropriate.

Adaptations

Adapting Programs for Specific Needs

Throughout this guide, an emphasis is placed on the importance of addressing the individual needs of each family when designing sleep interventions. Experience shows that compliance with sleep programs varies dramatically and particular attention needs to be made to differences in children as well as their families. This section highlights a few of the more common adaptations that are needed when developing intervention programs.

Age-Related Concerns

Children have different sleep needs at different ages. The chart in Module 2 provides a broad guideline for the average number of hours of sleep children need at different ages and this is used as a rule of thumb for gauging how much or how little a child should sleep. Several milestones related to the development of children are also useful to highlight since they can help guide treatment planning.

3 Months: Fading Nighttime Feedings

Most children do not need to be fed during the night after the age of about 3 months. This is important information for families of very young children because some parents believe the night waking and crying of their young child is the result of hunger, and they feel the need to continue these feedings. Unfortunately, nighttime feedings can lead to continued night waking because the child becomes conditioned to awaken at these times and, in turn, is conditioned to need the feeding to fall back asleep. Nighttime feedings after the age of 3 months can be faded according to the following schedule.

Fading Nighttime Feedings:

1. On the first night, instruct the parents to give the child feedings of 7 ounces (if bottle fed) or 7 minutes (if breast fed) with 2 hours between feedings.

2. On each subsequent night, the parents should reduce feedings by one ounce or minute (for example, the second night would be 6 ounces or minutes). They should also increase the time between feedings by 30 minutes (for example, from 2 hours to 2½ hours).

3. Remind families that a crying child may be hungry, but does not need the nourishment.

4. By the eighth night, the child should no longer be fed at bedtime or in the middle of the night.

6 Months: Sleeping Through the Night

Most infants can sleep through the night without awakening by the age of 6 months. This is a valuable guide for parents to have, because if their child is not sleeping through the night at this age, many parents feel that this is just a normal situation. In fact, we often find that telling parents this information gives them "permission" to begin to change the nighttime problems. If the child continues to awaken one or more times at night after having fallen asleep, and she is at least 6 months old, refer back to the previous modules for help in dealing with this problem.

5 years: Fading Daytime Naps

By age 2, children should be able to have an active morning without a nap. And somewhere between the ages of 3 and 6, most children no longer need an afternoon nap. Remember children are different when it comes to sleep needs. Some children and adults can nap during the day, and this does not negatively impact on their sleep. In contrast, other individuals who nap even for a short period of time can have trouble falling asleep at night or may awaken earlier than desired. At about the age of 5, if a child is still napping and this is interfering with sleep, then it may be time to begin to phase out this daytime sleeping. One helpful suggestion for families is that if they are going to awaken their child early from a nap, that they do it just before some favorite or fun activity (e.g., lunch time or play time) to reduce the child's irritability that sometimes occurs in these situations.

Teen Years: Accommodating Changes in Sleep Patterns

It has been estimated that after puberty, teens get about $7\frac{1}{2}$ hours of sleep each night, yet they need more than 9. At this time in development, the timing of sleep changes such that the pattern becomes delayed. Teens naturally begin to fall asleep later, and this is not just the result of late-night television watching or computer use. Unfortunately, most school districts schedule high school classes to begin at an early time, at the very point in development when this is problematic. This change in sleep patterns makes the sleep hygiene steps in Module 2 very important to follow during the teen years—especially the use of regular bedtimes and regular times to awaken.

Disorder-Related Concerns

The common developmental disorders observed in childhood (such as ADHD) typically are not associated with unique sleep problems. When children with other disorders have sleep problems, these are usually the same sleep disorders found among children without developmental disabilities. However, our experience shows us that concerns about the child's disorder often leads families to treat sleep problems differently— for example, going into the child's room more readily when sleep is disturbed. Anxiety in the family is often elevated around anything perceived to be unusual in the child's behavior and it is helpful to reassure these families that sleep problems are common among all children and that sleep treatments can be effective for their child. Sometimes, however, there are issues found among children with certain disorders that need to be addressed.

ADHD

The distractibility and the inability to stop thinking about worrisome issues (such as school or friendships) characteristic of children with ADHD can sometimes interfere with the ability of these children to fall asleep or fall back to sleep if awakened at night. At the same time, certain medications prescribed for ADHD can interfere with sleep. To address the "racing minds" of these children, several of the suggestions outlined in Module 5 for anxiety surrounding nightmares can be used. These techniques include using "magic" (for young children), relaxation training, and paradoxical intention. If stimulant medication is suspected as contributing to sleep disturbances, have the family consult with the prescribing physician to assess if alternative medications such as the non-stimulant antidepressant medications or melatonin would be useful.

One recommendation we often make is to allow a longer-than-usual bedtime routine for children who seem to need more time to wind down. After a few weeks of using a 1-hour bedtime routine that the child seems to accept, parents can decide if they want to shorten the time. Again, if this extra time seems to be interfering with sleep or is difficult to manage, we then help parents fade back the routine until it approximates the 30 minutes recommended. We do this slowly, by decreasing the routine from 60 to 50 minutes. If after two weeks the child has adapted to the 50-minute routine, we cut back the time to 40 minutes, and several weeks later if all is well, to 30 minutes. Fading back the bedtime routine often avoids fighting over bedtime, and lets the child slowly adapt to the restriction. Remind families that bedtime routines should be a calming time and not a time for conflict.

Epilepsy

Nighttime seizures can contribute to poor sleep in much the same way as interrupted breathing disrupts sleep. If the child has a history of seizures or she experiences daytime sleepiness but does not have breathing or limb movement problems (see Module 7), consider a medical referral.

Autism and Related Disorders

One word of caution about bedtime routines should be made for children with autism. Occasionally, these children adopt routines so strongly that they become rituals. For some children with autism, trying to vary the bedtime ritual even the slightest bit can result in a major tantrum. Parents of children with autism should be cautious when introducing new routines, and should consider building in variation, such as changing the order of the activities each night from the very beginning.

Disruptive Behavior

Problem behavior such as noncompliance, tantrums, and aggression accompany some of the developmental disorders. For sleep, this can manifest itself as bedtime or night-waking tantrums that have serious potential for doing harm to the child or that seriously disrupt the whole family each night. In these cases, we pay particular attention to recommending interventions that are "errorless"—meaning those that are less likely to result in disruption. Sleep restriction and scheduled awakening are two common interventions used when behavior surrounding sleep is unusually disruptive. Both of these treatments can usually be implemented with a minimum of disruption. Additionally, assistance for families in the use of behavioral interventions for daytime behavior problems is often warranted.

Cultural Concerns

When and where children sleep is, in part, culturally constructed. In many Western societies, it is expected that children will fall asleep in the early evening, in their own beds, and (when available) in their own rooms. However, this is not the case in other cultures and clinicians need to be sensitive to a family's cultural differences. Although not exhaustive, the following is a listing of important cultural differences that must be considered when designing plans (Jenni & O'Connor, 2005).

When Children Sleep

U.S.—Children of color will often go to bed later, get up later, and sleep less than white children.

Italy—Italian children have a shorter nightly sleep duration—going to bed later and waking up earlier—than children in the U.S.

Japan—Japanese children sleep less, sometimes napping after dinner but waking up to study late into the night.

Netherlands—Dutch infants sleep longer, going to bed earlier.

Bali—Balinese children may participate in occasional spiritual observances throughout the night and sleep on and off.

China— Chinese children's sleep changes seasonally, presumably to coincide with family work patterns.

Bedtime routines

Guatemala (Mayan), Spain, Greece and Italy—In these countries, there is no bedtime routine, and children are often allowed to fall asleep during family activities and then be put to bed.

Bali—Balinese infants are held all day long and sleep as needed.

Where Children Sleep

Italy—It is common for Italian children to sleep in the same room as the parents.

Japan—Japanese children often sleep in the same bed as parents.

Parental Sleep Concerns

Many sleep disorders are genetic and therefore it is expected that one or both parents will have significant sleep disturbances. At the same time, continued disruption of sleep by the child can lead to more persistent sleep disruption in the parents as well. Fortunately, the same interventions used for children can be effective for improving parental sleep problems.

Sleep hygiene is the first step in addressing adult sleep problems (Module 2) and it is important to include mention of alcohol use and smoking and their impact on sleep.

Alcohol Use

Alcohol consumed before bedtime—a common practice among adults to bring on drowsiness—can disrupt the second half of the sleep cycle, increasing episodes of partial waking. Alcohol use prior to bedtime can also increase interrupted breathing during sleep, which contributes to daytime drowsiness.

Smoking

The nicotine in cigarettes is a stimulant and, like caffeine, serves to stimulate the nervous system. Smoking right before bedtime can result in an overstimulation of the brain, which will interfere with sleep. Another problem for people who smoke is that to maintain their "fix" of nicotine, they need to smoke fairly often throughout the day. The problem they have with sleep is that they can experience "withdrawal" during the night, and this can disrupt sleep. It is not surprising that many smokers light up almost as soon as they wake up in the morning because their brains are craving nicotine. Parents should assess their smoking patterns to see if it is contributing to their disturbed sleep.

ALBANY SLEEP PROBLEMS SCALE (ASPS)

Name: _____ Date of Birth: _____

Diagnoses: _____ Sex: _____

Name of Respondent: _____ Date Adm: _____

Instructions: Circle *one* number that best represents the frequency of the behavior.

> 0 = Never
> 1 = Less than once per week
> 2 = One to two times per week
> 3 = Three to six times per week
> 4 = Nightly

1. Does the child have a fairly regular bedtime and time that he or she awakens? 0 1 2 3 4

2. Does the child have a bedtime routine that is the same each evening? 0 1 2 3 4

3. Does the child work or play in bed often right up to the time he or she goes to bed? 0 1 2 3 4

4. Does the child sleep poorly in his or her own bed, but better away from it? Yes No

5. Does the child consume caffeine in any form? 0 1 2 3 4

6. Does the child engage in vigorous activity in the hours before bedtime? 0 1 2 3 4

7. Does the child resist going to bed? 0 1 2 3 4

8. Does the child take more than 1 hour to fall asleep but does not resist? 0 1 2 3 4

9. Does the child awaken during the night but remain quiet and in bed? 0 1 2 3 4

10. Does the child awaken during the night and is he or she disruptive (e.g., tantrums, oppositional)? 0 1 2 3 4

11. Does the child take naps during the day? 0 1 2 3 4

12. Does the child often feel exhausted during the day because of lack of sleep? 0 1 2 3 4

13. Has the child ever had an accident or near accident because of sleepiness from not being able to sleep the night before? Yes No

14. Does the child ever use prescription drugs or over-the-counter medications to help him or her sleep? 0 1 2 3 4

15. Has the child found that sleep medication doesn't work as well as it did when he or she first started taking it? Yes No/NA

16. If taking sleep medication, does the child find that he or she can't sleep on nights without it?   Yes   No/NA

17. Does the child fall asleep early in the evening and awaken too early in the morning?   0   1   2   3   4

18. Does the child have difficulty falling asleep until a very late hour and difficulty awakening early in the morning?   0   1   2   3   4

19. Does the child wake up in the middle of the night upset?   0   1   2   3   4

20. Is the child relatively easy to comfort during these episodes?   Yes   No/NA

21. Does the child have episodes during sleep where he or she screams loudly for several minutes but is not fully awake?   0   1   2   3   4

22. Is the child difficult to comfort during these episodes?   Yes   No/NA

23. Does the child experience sleep attacks (falling asleep almost immediately and without warning) during the day?   0   1   2   3   4

24. Does the child experience excessive daytime sleepiness that is not due to an inadequate amount of sleep?   0   1   2   3   4

25. Does the child snore when asleep?   0   1   2   3   4

26. Does the child sometimes stop breathing for a few seconds during sleep?   0   1   2   3   4

27. Does the child have trouble breathing?   0   1   2   3   4

28. Is the child overweight?   Yes   No

29. Has the child often walked when asleep?   0   1   2   3   4

30. Does the child talk while asleep?   0   1   2   3   4

31. Are the child's sheets and blankets in extreme disarray in the morning when he or she wakes up?   0   1   2   3   4

32. Does the child wake up at night because of kicking legs?   0   1   2   3   4

33. While lying down, does the child ever experience unpleasant sensations in the legs?   Yes   No

34. Does the child rock back and forth or bang a body part (e.g., head) to fall asleep?   0   1   2   3   4

35. Does the child wet the bed?   0   1   2   3   4

36. Does the child grind his or her teeth at night?   0   1   2   3   4

37. Does the child sleep well when it doesn't matter, such as on weekends, but sleeps poorly when he or she "must" sleep well, such as when a busy day at school is ahead?   Yes   No

38. Does the child often have feelings of apprehension, anxiety, or dread when he or she is getting ready for bed?   0 1 2 3 4

39. Does the child worry in bed?   0 1 2 3 4

40. Does the child often have depressing thoughts, or do tomorrow's worries or plans buzz through his or her mind when he or she wants to go to sleep?   0 1 2 3 4

41. Does the child have feelings of frustration when he or she can't sleep?   0 1 2 3 4

42. Has the child experienced a relatively recent change in eating habits?   Yes   No

43. Does the child have behavior problems at times other than bedtime or upon awakening?   Yes   No

44. When did the child's primary difficulty with sleep begin?

_____

45. What was happening in the child's life at that time, or a few months before?

_____

46. Is the child under a physician's care for any medical condition? (If yes, indicate the condition below.)   Yes   No

OTHER COMMENTS:

_____

_____

_____

_____

_____

_____

_____

_____

_____

Sleep Intervention Questionnaire (SIQ)

Disruption Tolerance

1. Does your child misbehave at bedtime or when waking up at night in a way that is too serious or upsetting to ignore?

    Yes   No

2. Would it be difficult or impossible for you to listen to your child being upset for long periods of time (more than a few minutes)?

    Yes   No

3. Do you find it too difficult to put your child back in bed once he or she gets up?

    Yes   No

Schedule Tolerance

4. Are you, or another member of your family, willing to stay up later at night to put a sleep plan into action?

    Yes   No

5. Are you, or another member of your family, willing to get up earlier in the morning to put a sleep plan into action?

    Yes   No

Attitudinal Barriers

6. Do you feel emotionally unable to deal directly with your child's sleep problem?

    Yes   No

7. Do you feel guilty making your child go to bed (or go back to bed) when he or she does not want to?

    Yes   No

8. Do you think it would be emotionally damaging to your child if you tried to change the way he or she slept?

    Yes   No

Fidelity Checklists

Module 1: Pre-Intervention Assessment and Planning

Fidelity Checklist

Client Name: _____

Rate your fidelity to each session element on a scale of 1 to 7, with 1 indicating poor fidelity and 7 indicating high fidelity.

First Session: Sleep Interview and Assessment Tools   Date: _____

_____ Set agenda
_____ Provide information about sleep and its problems
_____ Administer the Albany Sleep Problems Scale (ASPS)
_____ Introduce Sleep Diary and Behavior Log
_____ Assign homework

Notes:

_____

_____

_____

Second Session: Data Analysis and Treatment Planning   Date: _____

_____ Set agenda
_____ Identify nature of sleep problems using results from ASPS
_____ Review parent's data from Sleep Diary
_____ Review parent's data from Behavior Log
_____ Provide information about sleep schedules and habits
_____ Administer the Sleep Intervention Questionnaire (SIQ)
_____ Discuss the results of the SIQ
_____ Discuss next steps
_____ Assign homework

Notes:

_____

_____

_____

Module 2: Good Sleep Hygiene

Fidelity Checklist

Client Name: _____

Rate your fidelity to each session element on a scale of 1 to 7, with 1 indicating poor fidelity and 7 indicating high fidelity.

First Session: Improving Sleep Hygiene   Date: _____

_____ Set agenda
_____ Review homework
_____ Discuss importance of good sleep habits
_____ Discuss age-related sleep needs
_____ Identify sleep hygiene problems and suggest changes
_____ Help family prioritize sleep hygienc issues
_____ Assign homework

Notes:

_____

_____

_____

_____

Follow-Up Sessions: Sleep Hygiene   Date: _____

_____ Set agenda
_____ Discuss family's progress since last session
_____ Discuss necessary modifications
_____ Address remaining sleep hygiene issues
_____ Assign homework

Notes:

_____

_____

_____

_____

Module 3: Bedtime

Fidelity Checklist

Client Name: _____

Rate your fidelity to each session element on a scale of 1 to 7, with 1 indicating poor fidelity and 7 indicating high fidelity.

First Session: Improving Bedtime   **Date:** _____

_____ Set agenda
_____ Review homework
_____ Describe intervention options for improving bedtime
_____ Select the appropriate intervention for the family
_____ Deal with family resistance, if necessary
_____ Present steps for graduated extinction (if selected intervention)
_____ Present steps for sleep restriction (if selected intervention)
_____ Assign homework

Notes:

_____

_____

_____

_____

Follow-Up Sessions: Bedtime Intervention   **Date:** _____

_____ Set agenda
_____ Discuss family's progress since last session
_____ Discuss necessary modifications
_____ Address remaining bedtime issues
_____ Assign homework

Notes:

_____

_____

_____

_____

Module 4: Night Waking

Fidelity Checklist

Client Name: _____

Rate your fidelity to each session element on a scale of 1 to 7, with 1 indicating poor fidelity and 7 indicating high fidelity.

First Session: Reducing Night Waking   **Date:** _____

- _____ Set agenda
- _____ Review homework
- _____ Describe intervention options for reducing night waking
- _____ Select the appropriate intervention for the family
- _____ Deal with family resistance, if necessary
- _____ Present steps for graduated extinction (if selected intervention)
- _____ Present steps for sleep restriction (if selected intervention)
- _____ Present steps for scheduled awakening (if selected intervention)
- _____ Assign homework

Notes:

_____

_____

_____

_____

Follow-Up Sessions: Night Waking Intervention   **Date:** _____

- _____ Set agenda
- _____ Discuss family's progress since last session
- _____ Discuss necessary modifications
- _____ Address remaining night waking issues
- _____ Assign homework

Notes:

_____

_____

_____

_____

Module 5: Nightmares and Sleep Terrors

Fidelity Checklist

Client Name: _____

Rate your fidelity to each session element on a scale of 1 to 7, with 1 indicating poor fidelity and 7 indicating high fidelity.

First Session: Reducing Nightmares and Sleep Terrors   Date: _____

_____ Set agenda
_____ Review homework
_____ Differentiate nightmares from sleep terrors
_____ Describe intervention options for reducing nightmares or sleep terrors
_____ Select the appropriate intervention for the family
_____ Deal with family resistance, if necessary
_____ Present steps for using "magic" (if selected intervention for nightmares)
_____ Present steps for relaxation (if selected intervention for nightmares)
_____ Present steps for paradoxical intention (if selected intervention for nightmares)
_____ Present steps for scheduled awakening (if selected intervention for sleep terrors)
_____ Assign homework

Notes:

_____

_____

_____

Follow-Up Sessions: Interventions for Nightmares and Sleep Terrors   Date: _____

_____ Set agenda
_____ Discuss family's progress since last session
_____ Discuss necessary modifications
_____ Address remaining issues with nightmares or sleep terrors
_____ Assign homework

Notes:

_____

_____

_____

_____

Module 6: Bedwetting

Fidelity Checklist

Client Name: _____

Rate your fidelity to each session element on a scale of 1 to 7, with 1 indicating poor fidelity and 7 indicating high fidelity.

First Session: Addressing Bedwetting   Date: _____

_____ Set agenda
_____ Introduce causes of bedwetting
_____ Instruct parents on initial steps
_____ Introduce Bedwetting Recording Sheet
_____ Assign homework

Notes:

_____

_____

Second Session: Reducing Bedwetting   Date: _____

_____ Set agenda
_____ Review homework
_____ Describe intervention options for bedwetting
_____ Select the appropriate intervention for the family
_____ Deal with family resistance, if necessary
_____ Present steps for the "bell and pad" technique
_____ Present steps for dry bed training
_____ Present steps for full-spectrum home training
_____ Discuss medical treatments for bedwetting
_____ Assign homework

Notes:

_____

_____

Follow-Up Sessions: Bedwetting Intervention   Date: _____

_____ Set agenda
_____ Discuss family's progress since last session
_____ Address remaining bedwetting issues
_____ Assign homework

Notes:

_____

_____

_____

Module 7: Other Sleep-Related Issues

Fidelity Checklist

Client Name: _____

Rate your fidelity to each session element on a scale of 1 to 7, with 1 indicating poor fidelity and 7 indicating high fidelity.

First Session: Improving Other Sleep-Related Problems   Date: _____

_____ Set agenda
_____ Review homework
_____ Differentiate and discuss other sleep-related problems
_____ Describe intervention options for reducing sleepwalking and related problems
_____ Describe intervention options for improving problems related to sleeping at the wrong times.
_____ Identify possible causes of excessive sleepiness
_____ Identify other nighttime problems or concerns
_____ Select the appropriate intervention for the family
_____ Assign homework

Notes:

_____

_____

_____

_____

Follow-Up Sessions: Interventions for Sleep-Related Problems   Date: _____

_____ Set agenda
_____ Discuss family's progress since last session
_____ Address remaining sleep-related issues
_____ Assign homework

Notes:

_____

_____

_____

_____

References

Adair, R., Bauchner, H., Philipp, B., Levenson, S., & Zuckerman, B. (1991). Night waking during infancy: Role of parent presence at bedtime. *Pediatrics, 87,* 500–504.

Anch, A.M., Browman, C.P., Mitler, M.M., & Walsh, J.K. (1988). *Sleep: A scientific perspective.* Englewood Cliffs, NJ: Prentice Hall.

Barclay, D.R., & Houts, A.C. (1995). Childhood enuresis. In C. E. Schaefer (Ed.), *Clinical handbook of sleep disorders in children* (pp. 223–252). Northvale, NJ: Jason Aronson Inc.

Blakeslee, S. (1993, August 3). Mystery of sleep yields as studies reveal immune tie. *The New York Times,* p. C1.

Carskadon, M.A., & Dement, W.C. (1989). Normal human sleep: An overview. In M.H. Kryer, T. Roth, & W.C. Dement (Eds.), *Principles and practice of sleep medicine* (pp. 3–13). Philadelphia: W.B. Saunders Company.

Christodulu, K.V., & Durand, V.M. (2004). Reducing bedtime disturbance and night waking using positive bedtime routines and sleep restriction. *Focus on Autism and Other Developmental Disabilities, 19,* 130–139.

Durand, V.M. (1998). *Sleep better!: A guide to improving sleep for children with special needs.* Baltimore, MD: Paul H. Brookes.

Durand, V.M. (2002). Treating sleep terrors in children with autism. *Journal of Positive Behavioral Interventions, 4,* 66–72.

Durand, V.M., & Christodulu, K.V. (2004). A description of a sleep restriction program to reduce bedtime disturbances and night waking. *Journal of Positive Behavioral Interventions, 6,* 83–91.

Durand, V.M., Gernert-Dott, P., & Mapstone, E. (1996). Treatment of sleep disorders in children with developmental disabilities. *Journal of The Association for Persons with Severe Handicaps, 21,* 114–122.

Durand, V. M., & Mindell, J. A. (1990). Behavioral treatment of multiple childhood sleep disorders: Effects on child and family. *Behavior Modification, 14,* 37–49.

Durand, V.M., & Mindell, J.A. (1999). Behavioral intervention for childhood sleep terrors. *Behavior Therapy, 30,* 705–715.

Durand, V.M., Mindell, J., Mapstone, E., & Gernert-Dott, P. (1995). Treatment of multiple sleep disorders in children. In C. E. Schaefer (Ed.), *Clinical handbook of sleep disorders in children* (pp. 311–333). Northvale, NJ: Jason Aronson Inc.

Giles, D.E., & Buysse, D.J. (1993). Parasomnias. In D.L. Dunner (Ed.), *Current psychiatric therapy* (pp. 361–372). Philadelphia: W.B. Saunders Company.

Hauri, P. (1982). *The sleep disorders* (2nd ed.). Kalamazoo, MI: Upjohn Company.

Jenni, O. G., & O'Connor, B. B. (2005). Children's sleep: An interplay between culture and biology. *Pediatrics, 115*(1), 204–216.

Makari, J., & Rushton, H.G. (2006). Nocturnal enuresis. *American Family Physician, 73,* 1611–1618.

Mindell, J.A., & Durand, V.M. (1993). Treatment of childhood sleep disorders: Generalization across disorders and effects on family members. *Journal of Pediatric Psychology, 18,* 731–750.

Mindell, J. A., Emslie, G., Blumer, J., Genel, M., Glaze, D., Ivanenko, A., Johnson, K., Rosen, C., Steinberg, F., Roth, T., & Banas, B. (2006). Pharmacologic management of insomnia in children and adolescents: Consensus statement. *Pediatrics, 117*(6), 1223–1232.

Oredsson, A. F., & Jorgensen, T. M. (1998). Changes in nocturnal bladder capacity during treatment with the bell and pad for monosymptomatic nocturnal enuresis. *The Journal of Urology, 160*(1), 166–169.

Owens, J.A. (2005). The ADHD and sleep conundrum: A review. *Developmental and Behavioral Pediatrics, 26,* 312–322.

Owens, J. A., Rosen, C. L., & Mindell, J. A. (2003). Medication use in the treatment of pediatric insomnia: results of a survey of community-based pediatricians. *Pediatrics, 111*(5 Pt 1), e628–635.

Palmblad, J., Petrini, B., Wasserman, J., & Akerstedt, T. (1979). Lymphocyte and granulocyte reactions during sleep deprivation. *Psychosomatic Medicine, 41,* 273–278.

Rechtschaffen, A., & Foulkes, D. (1965). Effect of visual stimuli on dream content. *Perceptual and Motor Skills, 20,* 1149–1160.

Rolider, A., & Van Houten, R. (1984). Training parents to use extinction to eliminate nighttime crying by gradually increasing the criteria for ignoring crying. *Education and Treatment of Children, 7,* 119–124.

Safarinejad, M. R. (in press). Prevalence of nocturnal enuresis, risk factors, associated familial factors and urinary pathology among school children in Iran. *Journal of Pediatric Urology.*

Spielman, A. J. & Glovinsky, P. B. (1991). The varied nature of insomnia. In P. Hauri (Ed.), *Case studies in insomnia* (pp. 1–15). Plenum Press, New York.

About the Author

V. Mark Durand, PhD, is currently professor of psychology at the University of South Florida St. Petersburg. He served in several administrative roles over the past decade, including founding Dean of Arts & Sciences and the Regional Vice Chancellor for Academic Affairs. Durand previously was on the faculty at the University of Albany—The State University of New York, where he received the University Award for Excellence in Teaching and founded the Albany Center for Autism and Related Disabilities in the mid 1990s. Dr. Durand is a Fellow of the American Psychological Association and has administered more than $4 million in federal research and training grants.

His published work includes numerous books and over 100 other research publications. One book—*Severe Behavior Problems: A Functional Communication Training Approach*—is the product of 10 years of empirical research and outlines a novel treatment for problem behavior using communication. He developed the *Motivation Assessment Scale,* a functional behavioral assessment instrument that is now translated into 15 languages. He has also authored several bestselling textbooks, including *Abnormal Psychology: An Integrative Approach*, and published the first book on sleep disorders for children with disabilities—*Sleep Better!: A Guide to Improving Sleep for Children with Special Needs.* Dr. Durand serves on the editorial boards of several journals including *Clinical Psychology Review, Journal of Developmental and Physical Disabilities, Journal of Positive Behavioral Interventions,* and *Focus on Autism and Other Developmental Disabilities.* He was recently elected to the Board of Professional Advisors for the Autism Society of America.